PROMISE
OF
HOPE

DEVOTIONS FOR PRISONERS

GEORGE FITZGERALD

DEVOTIONS FOR PRISONERS

Promise of Hope - Devotions for Prisoners
Copyright © 2007 by George Fitzgerald

Requests for information should be sent to:

ReBuild International Group, LLC
PO Box 12162
Norfork VA 23541

Cover Design by Michael Dolan

Published By LuLu
www.Lulu.com

ISBN: 978-1-4357-0783-2

Printed in the United States of America.

PROMISE
OF
HOPE

Dedication

I dedicate this book to my wife, Ruth, who is the epitome of a Proverbs 31 woman. Her encouragement for me to write has finally paid off, to the glory of God. I thank the Lord for blessing me with this jewel from heaven. She has definitely been a pillar of support to me during our entire marriage. As the Proverb says "... her children rise up and call her blessed. Her husband also and he praises her. Many daughters have done well, but she excels them all."

The passion that she has for ministry to those incarcerated whether in jails, prisons, mental hospitals or juvenile homes is phenomenal. The compassion she has for people in general warms the <u>hearts</u> of everyone who comes in contact with her. I'm blessed to have her and wouldn't put anyone (other than Jesus) or anything above her. She's my wife, my sister, my partner in ministry, my lover and friend.

This one's for you babe,

George Fitzgerald

ACKNOWLEDGMENTS

Special Thanks ...

To our Lord and Savior, Jesus Christ for making all of this possible.

... Our children, Everett, Erika, Manu, Timika, Maceo, Jorgina and Naomi; our grandchildren, Ahja, Jhana, Rheya, Xavian, Zion, Israel and Logan; because of you we purpose to live a godly life and establish a godly inheritance so that you may prosper in every area of your lives.

... Dr. Ronald and Donna Fuhrmann, for your demonstration of the love of God during the most difficult times of our lives – we are eternally grateful. You are the epitome of friendship. Thanks for holding our hands.

... Bob and Cindy Hopkins, Rhonda & DeArmond Mathews, Zebbe Dee Hernandez, Sherry and Anthony Hicks, Larry Davis, Jody Pinckney, Deborah Butler, Marc and Gessie Thompson, Keith and Sara Davis, Rev. Keith and Barbara Pettus, Charles and Cynthia Whitehead, Yvonne Harris, Gary Turner, Jannette Watts, CeCe McCall, Rene and Teresa Lockhart, Pastor Bob, Bruce and Camella Binkley, for your words of encouragement, prayers, support and most of all, your love.

... My spiritual son, Pastor Martin Nangoli and Wake Up Ministry Uganda for laboring in the prisons and bringing a promise of hope.

... Mary Taylor for her labor of love in editing this devotion.

... Sarah Hamilton and Michael Dolan – we are eternally grateful for your gift of service. You have blessed us and those who will be drawn to read this book.

... To all of the hidden treasures of darkness hidden behind prison walls and those that are release – that we have had the opportunity to minister to and disciple, you have given us a promise of hope!

PREFACE

Why "120" daily devotions in the Promise of Hope, some may ask? Well, at first I wanted to do "365", one for each day of the year, but the Holy Spirit impressed the number "120" upon my heart, and I couldn't shake it. So I inquired of God, why this number? As He began to break it down for me, there was no longer any doubt or questioning the number "120."

First, he showed me that "120" was the number that was needed to form a council in any Jewish city. Plus, twelve, which is the number of organization multiplied by ten--the number of completion--equals one hundred and twenty. So "120" is definitely a complete organizational structure. Remember that there were "120" in the upper room (Acts 1:15).

Secondly, we know that there were "12" tribes of Israel and "12" disciples (Matthew 10:1-5), who were also the "12" apostles. Then there were "12" thrones for the "12" tribes as well as "12" gates to the Holy City (Revelation 21:12, 21) and "12" foundations for the Holy City (Revelation 21:14). Remember, too, that Jesus in Matthew 26:53 could have commissioned more than "12" legions of angels to come to His rescue. So we can see that "12" is the organizational structure of God.

Thirdly, when we look at "10" as being the completeness of God, we see its proof in the "10" commandments (Exodus 34:28) and the "10" days of testing that Daniel and his three friends went through (Daniel 1:12, 14-15). Next we see completeness described in the parable of the "10" virgins (Matthew 25:1); the "10" lepers (Luke 17:12, 17), and what about the "10" days of tribulations found in Revelation 2:10? Then there are the "10" thousand saints that the Lord brings with Him to execute judgment on all (Jude 14, 15). Though there are numerous more examples of "ten" representing the completeness of God, this should suffice for now.

Fourthly, the Lord showed me the significance of both "40" and "3". "Forty" not only represented a time of preparation, but also a time of cleansing. That's why the earth/world went through "40" days and nights of rain, so that it could be cleansed and then prepared for a new generation. Also the same principle applied to the "40" years of the Israelites wandering around in the wilderness. One generation had to be removed (cleansed), while preparations for a new one could be made simultaneously. Other examples of this principle are found with Moses on the Mount (Exodus 24:18), the spies searching out Canaan land (Numbers 13), Moses' time of fasting (Deuteronomy 9:18) and Elijah's flight from Jezebel (1 Kings 19:8). Though Jesus also experienced "40" days and nights of fasting and prayer, I believe that His example was more figurative than physical. I make this premise on the fact that there was no need for Him to be cleansed since He was without sin. (Matthew 4:2)

PREFACE

Finally, the number three is one of the greatest numbers in the Bible, mainly because God is a triune God, - Father, Son and Holy Spirit. He also has created man to be a triune being which is body, soul and spirit. There is so much that I could share about God and how He operates in the third dimension and how He wants us to operate in that dimension, but it would be too lengthy. So you, dear reader, will have to wait for my upcoming book "Third Dimension."

For now, I just want to share with you a few examples of how God is not only a triune God, but also does everything in "threes" to show you the importance of the number "three." Jesus said, "At the mouth of two or three witnesses let every matter be established." (Matthew 18:16) Jesus was raised on the third day. Daniel fasted and prayed for "three weeks." (Daniel 10:2,3) Jonah was in the belly of the whale for "three" days. (Jonah 1:17) The apostle Paul was caught up to the third heavens. (2 Corinthians 12:2) In the tabernacle there were "three" separate compartments (the outer court, the inner court and the Holy of Holies), and each section had "three" items of furniture in it. There are three things in heaven that bear witness: the Father, the Son and the Holy Spirit. (1 John 5:7) I could go on with many more examples, but I believe that the point has been made. So because the number "three" helps to establish a matter and places emphasis on it, I felt led to have it multiplied by "40," consequently giving me confirmation for "120" devotions – "Promise of Hope."

Also, I want to encourage every reader to study and meditate upon these "Promises of Hope" at least "three" times, which would take them through the whole year. The more you meditate upon the "Promise of Hope," the more the principles will get in your spirit. Before you know it, you will not only be encouraged but also growing spiritually.

Share the "Promise of Hope" with your friends and families. Remember that the promises were written with the prison population and their families in mind. So if you are close to someone who is presently incarcerated or on probation or parole, share the "Promise of Hope" with them and their family members.

FOREWORD

This devotion was birthed during a time of adversity -- at a crossroads of life where all hell had broken loose. George and I had a decision to make: Shall we go forward, or shall we die? Will we continue to trust God for our lives – our hope and our future?

I had been walking with God for nineteen years in September 2004, when God spoke to me and said, "Enough is enough." These words still ring loud and clear as I finish this manuscript, and each day it becomes clearer why we experienced what we did. George and I had been called for such a time as this to bring those out of darkness into His marvelous light. And God has purposed that it shall be! So whatever has taken place because of our disobedience and man's plans to destroy – God is still in control, and His plan shall not be thwarted.

As I sat in the midst of my pain, anger rose and the thought came, "Let's turn what was meant for evil into good." (Genesis 50:20) Let's use this time of being in the wilderness to become vessels God can use to be a blessing to another in pain. Let's put together a devotional for those who have been forgotten and have no hope, and who better to do that than George and Ruth!

I know that the Lord has spared our lives and given us another opportunity to bring "Promise of Hope" to those behind prison walls around the world. Also, He has granted us an opportunity to provide their loved ones with a resource to assist in the rebuilding of their lives and their relationship with the Lord.

It is my prayer that every soul that reads this devotional will truly be inspired and will know just how much the Lord loves them and has not forgotten them; that they will give up the ways of the world and the culture inside of the prison to become the men and women of God He has created them to be.

This is the beginning of a new season for those imprisoned behind prison walls and time for revival to begin as they get to know God and recognize that they have been set aside by God to do great and mighty exploits for Him.

Galatians 6:1 tells us, "Brethren, if a man be overtaken in a fault, ye which are spiritual, restore such a one in the spirit of meekness; considering thyself, lest thou also be tempted." "Promise of Hope" is written to restore those who were overtaken in a fault.

Lord, thank you that You spared George's life, and Your Hand kept him during his time of destruction, and Your mercy triumphed over judgment in his life. And Your grace is sustaining him in his hour of need. Your Love is amazing!

Ruth Fitzgerald

*This is what the Lord says: I will answer your prayers
because I have set a time when I will help
by coming to save you.
I have chosen you to take my*
promise of hope
*to other nations.
You will rebuild the country from its ruins,
then people will come and settle there.
You will set prisoners free from dark dungeons
to see the light of day.*

*On their way home, they will find plenty to eat,
even on barren hills.
They won't go hungry or get thirsty;
they won't be bothered by the scorching sun
or hot desert winds.
I will be merciful while leading them along
to streams of water.
I will level the mountains and make roads.
Then my people will return from distant lands
in the north and the west
and from the city of Syene."*

Isaiah 49:8-12

Day 1

"Entering and Leaving"

Matthew 10:11-14

"And into whatsoever city or town ye shall enter, inquire who in it is worthy; and there abide till ye go thence. And when ye come into an house, salute it. And if the house be worthy, let your peace come upon it; but if it be not worthy, let your peace return to you. And whatsoever shall not receive you, nor hear your words, when ye depart out of that house or city, shake off the dust of your feet."

Not many saints are familiar with the concept and pattern of "entering and leaving." Yet one of the first principles I've learned under the tutelage of my spiritual mentor, Dr. Edwin Louis Cole, was that "all life is lived on levels and arrived at in stages." He explained that how we leave one level or stage determines how we will enter the next. Yes, our whole life is a series (cycle) of entering & leaving. For instance, we leave the womb and enter infancy; leave infancy and enter childhood; leave childhood and enter adolescence, leave adolescence and enter adulthood. We leave school and enter the workforce. We leave singleness and enter marriage! And the list and cycles go on and on. The key is that how we leave will determine how we enter. For example, if you leave one relationship on a negative level with a whole lot of baggage, then you will enter the next relationship with that same baggage.

As we enter into a new year, let's purpose in our hearts not to bring the baggage from the previous year. Let's leave the past year on a positive note so that we can enter a new year on a positive note.

Remember Jesus said, "...whatever city or town you enter, seek who is worthy and stay there till you go out." Let your peace come upon that household. But if they don't receive you than depart (leave) that house or city, and shake the dust from your feet." (Scripture notation)

Soul Check

What kind of baggage are you still carrying?

Confession

I am shaking the dust off my feet, leaving the past and entering into the new.

Day 2

"Say It Loud"

Acts 4:29-31

And now, Lord, behold their threatenings: and grant unto thy servants, that with all boldness they may speak thy word. By stretching forth thine hand to heal; and that signs and wonders may be done by the name of the holy child Jesus. And when they had prayed, the place was shaken where they were assembled together; and they were all filled with the Holy Ghost, and they spake the word of God with boldness.

Before the disciples in the first century were ever called "Christians" (Acts 11:26) in Antioch, they were simply known as those who belong to the "Way". (Acts 9:2) However, they were exemplifying the characteristics and conduct of Christ so much until they started calling them Christians. Neither were they shy about sharing the Word. As recorded in Acts 4:29, 31, they even prayed for more boldness to speak God's Word after they were threatened.

Back in the late Sixties, "The Godfather of Soul", James Brown, had a hit record called "Say It Loud, I'm Black and I'm Proud." So many African Americans, (believers included) shouted whenever they could, "Say It Loud, I'm Black and I'm Proud." But I encourage all believers to "Say It Loud, I'm a Christian and I'm Proud."

We need to stop letting the enemy push us into a closet and, like the Apostles, pray for more boldness to declare who we are and the Word of God, both through our actions and our conduct. Especially in prisons and jails around the country, we need to stop being ashamed to be identified with Christ. That's what Christians are all about: "being like Christ." So men and women of God, let them know that the days of concealing our Bibles under our jackets and meeting in seclusion are over. From now on, in the Name of Jesus, under the anointing of the Holy Spirit, we are "Saying it Loud, We're Christians and we're Proud."

Soul Check

Are you saying it loud, or are you in the closet?

Confession

I am saying it loud – I am a Christian and I am proud!

Day 3

"In The Way"

Matthew 16:24-27

Then Jesus said unto his disciples, If any man will come after me, let him deny himself, and take up his cross, and follow me. For whosoever will save his life shall lose it: and whosoever will lose his life for my sake shall find it. For what is a man profited, if he shall gain the whole world, and lose his own soul? Or what shall a man give in exchange for his soul? For the Son of man shall come in the glory of his father with his angels, and then he shall reward every man according to his works.

It's amazing how a cliché from one generation will always come back around to another, much like fashions and fads. When I was growing up, if an adult (related or not) said that you are "in the way", it meant that you had better move on to a safer, less hostile environment, because, you definitely were in their way. However, today's version of being "in the way" takes on a whole new meaning. What it means for those growing up in our urban society as well as in the sub-culture of our jails and prisons is that you are hindering one from obtaining something or accomplishing a goal. It always has a negative connotation, just as it did when I was coming up. If they perceive that you have said or done something to keep them from making progress, then you are "in the way."

Well, I believe that the text in Matthew 16:24-27 can be paraphrased to say that we are in the way when it comes to Jesus and spiritual things. We are so much in the way until it sometimes takes an earth-shaking experience to move us out of the way. The only way we will ever achieve the spiritual life, the abundant life, even the glorified life, is to let the Holy Spirit move us out of the way. The last thing we want, my beloved saints, is for Jesus to say to us, "You're in the way."

Lord, help us to fulfill today's text in our daily walk with You.

Soul Check

Are you "In the way?"

Confession

I am getting out of the way. Have your way, Lord.

Day 4

"Welcome Home, Backslider!"

Jeremiah 3:22-25

Return , ye backsliding children, and I will heal your backslidings. Behold, we come unto thee; for thou art the Lord our God. Truly in vain is salvation hoped for from the hills, and from the multitude of mountains: truly in the Lord our God is the salvation of Israel. For shame hath devoured the labour of our fathers from our youth; their flocks and their herds, their sons and their daughters.

1 John 1:9

If we confess our sins, he is faithful and just to forgive us our sins, and to cleanse us from all unrighteousness.

If I had to give an educated guess about the percentage of backslidden Christians in our jails and prisons, I would say it is probably around seventy to eighty percent. Pretty high, one might think, but once they open to you, you'll find that most of the prisoners grew up in the church. Plus, they really love God but don't want to go back to the kind of traditional church that hurt them or condemned them. Some even think that they have committed the unpardonable sin. Well, I want to encourage that person to come back to the Lord today. Read the Scriptures for today, and let them penetrate your heart and spirit. For I say to you today that as long as you confess your sins, God is faithful and just to forgive you. And not only will He forgive you, but He also will cleanse you of all unrighteousness. So forget about what others may say or think about you; it doesn't matter. What they say and think doesn't determine who you are; it's what God says and thinks about you that is important. Don't let anyone or anything keep you from walking in the blessings of God. Stop looking at man, who will always hurt or disappoint you, and start looking to Jesus, the Author and Finisher of our faith. (Hebrews 12:2). He will never fail you, hurt you or disappoint you. Confess those sins out of your life, and confess His righteousness in. Welcome home, backslider!

Soul Check

Are you a backslider?

Confession
I am returning to the family of God. I confess my sins and confess His righteousness in me. I will look unto Jesus, the author and finisher of my faith. I am no longer backslidden.

Day 5

"Dress To Impress"

Ephesians 6:13-17 The Promise CEV

So put on all the armor that God gives. Then when that evil day comes, you will be able to defend yourself. And when the battle is over, you will be standing firm. Be ready! Let the truth be like a belt around your waist, and let God's justice protect you like armor. Your desire to tell the good news about peace should be like shoes on your feet. Let your faith be like a shield, and you will be able to stop all the flaming arrows of the evil one. Let God's saving power be like a helmet, and for a sword use God's message that comes from the Spirit.

Has it ever dawned on you just how much time we spend in front of the mirror? Or how careful we are to pick out the right clothes for that particular day? And sometimes, once we are fully dressed and almost out the door, all of a sudden we don't like the way we look or feel, so we eventually end up changing our whole ensemble. As humorous as it sounds, some of us are guilty of changing two or three times, even though that's the extent of our wardrobe. We want to look good and deserve to look good so that we can feel good about ourselves. However, sometimes we spend more time putting on natural clothes that we don't have to time to put on our spiritual clothes, what the Bible calls our "spiritual armor". Well, it's just as important as our natural clothes and far more valuable! Have you ever noticed that five parts of our spiritual armor are defensive protection armor, while only the sword of the spirit is for the offensive.

The <u>helmet</u> for the head in various forms embossed with many kinds of figures.
The <u>girdle</u> for the loins to brace the armor tight against the body and provide support from daggers, swords and other weapons.
The <u>breastplate</u> in two parts: one to cover the breast and the other to cover the back to protect the vital organs of the body. It extended down to the legs.
The brazen <u>boots</u> for the feet to cover the front of the legs. Finally, the <u>shield</u> to protect the body from blows and cuts.

Now that's what I call "Dress to Impress". Put on the whole armor each day.

Soul Check

Are you dressed in the whole armor of God today?

Confession

I will "dress to impress" by putting on the whole armor of God.

Day 6

"What's Love Got to Do with It?"

John 13:34-35

A new commandment I give unto you, that ye love one another; as I have loved you, that ye also love one another. By this shall all men know that ye are my disciples, if ye have love one to another.

Most of us have heard Tina Turner belt out this song from the top of her lungs, while Fat Joe used it for the hook (sample) to one of his rap songs. And they even made a movie about it. Yet, none have even come close to what the real answer is. So I submit to you today that spiritually and relationally, "love has everything to do with it." Love should be the core of our very lives and the relationships that we develop. Love is the most valuable commodity that we have, and yet so many of us take it for granted. We haven't learned the different types of love, so we often don't operate in them to our fullest potential. For instance, the Bible uses three different terms that are translated "love" in our English language:

(1) Phileo, which denotes a brotherly love and this is where we get our word "Philadelphia" from.

(2) Storge, which is a love based on natural affections (as noted in 2 Timothy 3:3).

(3) Agape, which is the kind of love our Heavenly Father has for us and wants us to have for our neighbors. Agape love is the one that is based on principles and not emotions. It's unconditional, redemptive and sacrificial.

What about Eros, where we get our word <u>erotic</u> from? Well, it's not even mentioned in the Bible. Eros is based on physical attraction only, and most people have experienced this type of love. So what's love got to do with it? I'd say "everything," based on our Scriptures for today and the manner in which the Lord commands us to love!

Additional Reading: Matthew 19:19, Proverbs 10:12, 1 Corinthians 13:1-13

Soul Check
Are you walking in love?

Confession
I will love as commanded by the Word of God.

Day 7

"Master Garbage Collector"

Mark 11:15-17

And they come to Jerusalem : and Jesus went into the temple, and began to cast out them that sold and bought in the temple, and overthrew the tables of the moneychangers, and the seats of them that sold doves; And would not suffer that any man should carry any vessel through the temple. And he taught, saying unto them, Is it not written, My house shall be called of all nations the house of prayer? But ye have made it a den of thieves.

When we study the life of Jesus, especially the last three and half years of His ministry, we see a lot of what He accomplished. Much of His job description can be equated with the titles He held. For instance, we know for certain that He was prophet, priest and king and walked in those offices during His ministry. We also know that He was a healer and deliverer, for He went about healing all sorts of sickness and diseases, as well as, delivering those who were possessed by demons. See Matthew 4:23-25. However, did you know that He was also a "Master Garbage Collector?" In the Scriptures for today, the word many commentators use for this cleaning of the temple is purification. Purification is a process of taking out the impurities in something or someone, and leaving that which is pure. I like to think of it as a process of collecting all of the garbage out of my life and leaving only that which lines up with His Word and His Will. All of us have some garbage in our lives that we've been praying to have removed. Well, Jesus is saying that "despite all of the glorious titles He holds, Master Garbage Collector eats at Him the most." He gets emotionally intense when His Father's House is contaminated. We are the temples of the Most Holy One, so let's allow Him to collect the garbage out of our lives. What I really like about the Mark account is that after He threw the moneychangers out, He then stood at the entrance and wouldn't let them back in.

Additional reading: Matthew 21:12-16, John 2:13-16

Soul Check

What garbage do you have in your life?

Confession

Master Garbage Collector, you have my permission to remove the garbage out of my life so that I can line up with Your Word and Your Will.

Day 8

"Spiritual Dream Team"

1 John 5:7

For there are three that bear record in heaven, the Father, the Word, and the Holy Ghost; and these three are one.

A few years ago when the Olympic Committee decided to let professional basketball players from the U.S. join the Olympic Game, man, did we pick a team! The team was the first ever to go undefeated in all of their games and won the gold metal. We called them the "Dream Team." I don't recall off the top of my head who all the players were, but I'm sure that any sports buff could find out. Then came the legal "Dream Team" for Mr. O.J. Simpson - a team of the best lawyers that money could ever buy. We all know the end of that legal battle, so let's move on. We saw the Dream Team for sports and legal entities, but now, let's look at the "Spiritual Dream Team" that we all can have representing us. Because we have Almighty God Himself, His Son Jesus, and the Holy Spirit on the "Dream Team", we too can go undefeated in every area of our lives. Plus, no matter how many cases or legal battles come against us, we can win them all with the "Dream Team" we have. Dream Teams in the natural are fallible and subject to constant change. Also a team is assembled based on competition, with the twelve best getting the nod. Well, our "Dream Team" is infallible, not put together based on competition, and it never changes. (read Hebrews 13:5, 8.) Thank God for this Dream Team that not only represents us now, but for all eternity. How can we lose with the stuff that they use?

Thank you Father, Son and Holy Spirit.

Soul Check

Whose team are you on?

Confession

I am represented by the Father, Son and Holy Spirit "Dream Team;" therefore I will never lose.

Day 9

"Change"

2 Corinthians 3:18

But we all, with open face beholding as in a glass the glory of the Lord, are changed into the same image from glory to glory, even as by the Spirit of the Lord.

Change isn't change until it is changed. Everyone knows that some areas in their lives need to be changed, but they are fearful of making a change. Nobody likes a change (except a baby), mainly for fear of the unexpected. So people adapt to their situation and/or circumstances and become comfortable in them. However, whether we want to change or accept change, it really is the only constant in our lives. Nobody or nothing stays the same. All of God's creation is subject to change. Change isn't bad or evil; it's necessary to get us from one level or stage in life to the next one. God wants us to accept change and make progress as He takes us from faith to faith, and glory to glory; as He builds precept upon precept. There's no stagnation in life; you either progress or regress, but you will move one way or the other. As I've stated before, we may not like to change, but it is necessary for our growth. The only time change is negative is when we regress rather than progress. Sometimes the change is gradual or sometimes it's instant. The changes we make need to be spiritual first and then physical. God wants to transform us into the image of His Son. Transformation is change. Change makes us better, especially when the change is initiated by God.

Additional reading: Isaiah 28:10, Romans 1:17

Soul Check

Are you ready to change?

Confession

I am no longer fearful about change. Lord, change me!

Day 10

"R – U – MADD"

Matthew 5:13-16

Ye are the salt of the earth: but if the salt have lost his savour, wherewith shall it be salted? It is thenceforth good for nothing, but to be cast out, and to be trodden under foot of men. Ye are the light of the world. A city that is set on an hill cannot be hid. Neither do men light a candle, and put it under a bushel, but on a candlestick; and it giveth light unto all that are in the house. Let your light so shine before men that they may see your good works, and glorify your Father which is in heaven.

I once heard Bishop Dale C. Bronner from Atlanta, Georgia, refer to a message he had recently preached, asking his congregation were they MAD. Not having heard the message, I was bewildered, as were any other visitors that Sunday morning. Once he explained the acronym, I immediately knew that I would be using it at some point in the future. The acronym stood for "Making A Difference." I took the liberty to add a "D" to MAD so that the acronym would now stand for "Making A Difference Daily." I believe that the Lord wants us to make a difference in people's lives on a daily basis. So my question to you that are striving to live holy lives behind the walls of jails and prisons is, "Are you making a difference daily?" I know that it's often difficult because of all the distractions, as well as the close quarters we live in. But thanks be to God, we can be successful if we don't give up. How do you make a difference daily in this type of environment? Well, for one, let your light shine, your speech be seasoned with salt, and your conduct above reproach. Discipline yourself in spiritual things such as reading the Word daily, praying, fasting, having devotions and Bible studies. As you discipline yourself in the Word, changes will happen in your life that will make others take notice and say, "God truly is with him." So as you walk in love and dress in the complete armour of God, you will "make a difference daily!"

Soul Check

Are you making a difference?

Confession

I am making a difference daily. I am MADD!

Day 11

"Maximized Manhood"

Joel 3:9

Proclaim ye this among the Gentiles; Prepare war, wake up the mighty men, let all the men of war draw near; let them come up.

Ben Kinchlow said it best when he coined the phrase "Being a male is a matter of birth, while being a man is a matter of choice!" You see, we are born either male or female, but we grow up to be men and women. A spiritual definition of being a man is "Christlike-ness and manhood are synonymous." Simply put, to be a man is to be like Christ. But the text says "... the mighty men ..." Yes, the text says "mighty men," to differentiate between mighty men and the three other types of men in the world today. Most people in the world, especially in jails and prisons, don't even realize that there is a difference in the types of men, so consequently they sometimes end up being the wrong type, the type that the Lord can't use. Most males will develop or define their manhood based on the type of role models and environment that they grew up with. In our next four days of devotions, we are going to look at the four types of men so that you can correctly appreciate what kind of man you are. You see, God's ultimate goal is to wake up the mighty man so that He can "... pour out His Spirit upon him ... "(Joel 2:28, 29) and then bring restoration in his life and every area that pertains to his life. (Joel 2:25) All of us need some restoration.

Soul Check

Are you a mighty man?

Confession

I am awake, and I am a mighty man.

Day 12

"Macho Men"

Joel 2:25-28

And I will restore to you the years that the locust hath eaten, the cankerworm, and the caterpillar and the palmerworm, my great army which I sent among you. And ye shall eat in plenty, and be satisfied, and praise the name of the Lord your God, that hath dealt wondrously with you: and my people shall never be ashamed. And ye shall know that I am in the midst of Israel, and that I am the Lord your God, and none else: and my people shall never be ashamed. And it shall come to pass afterward, that I will pour out my spirit upon all flesh; and your sons and daughters shall prophesy, your old men shall see visions.

Macho men are the first type of men that we will discuss. Macho men are the type of men who base their manhood on several different factors. First, because of their low self-esteem and insecurity, they base their manhood on how much money they have in their pockets or how much they can dominate a woman. Secondly, many macho men have complexes and unresolved issues that haven't been dealt with, so they walk around projecting an image that they are real tough, when in reality they really aren't. A lot of image projection is done in the jails and prisons. Many at the first sign of conflict will vocalize how much of a man they are though no one ever questioned their manhood. But no matter how much they project a tough guy image, the real self will surface in time, especially in a controlled environment. Lastly, many like to base their manhood on how many babies they make. Well, any dog can have a litter of pups, but it still won't make him a man. God doesn't want us to be macho men - so if you have been or still are a macho man, don't fret, because there is help. Remember, to be a man is to be like Christ. Through Him, you too can "put off the old man and put on the new man."

Additional reading: Ephesians 4:22-24

Soul Check

Are you a macho man?

Confession

I am putting off the old man and putting on the new man.

Day 13

"Marshmallow Men"

Joel 2:25-29

And I will restore to you the years that the locust hath eaten, the cankerworm, and the caterpillar and the palmerworm, my great army which I sent among you. And ye shall eat in plenty, and be satisfied, and praise the name of the Lord your God that hath dealt wondrously with you: and my people shall never be ashamed. And ye shall know that I am in the midst of Israel and that I am the Lord your God, and none else: and my people shall never be ashamed. And it shall come to pass afterward, that I will pour out my spirit upon all flesh; and your sons and daughters shall prophesy, your old men shall see visions: And also upon the servants and upon the handmaids in those days will I pour my spirit.

The second kind of men comes from the group called "Marshmallow Men." This group has no backbone or inner strength, so they become men of preference as opposed to men of conviction. They tend to waver back and forth from one opinion to another. They are what the Bible describes as "being tossed to and fro with every wind of doctrine, by the trickery of men in the cunning craftiness of deceitful plotting." (Ephesians 4:14) Because they have no backbone and no strong conviction for their foundation, they tend to base their manhood on whatever is the flavor of the month. In jails and prisons "Marshmallow Men" become a Christian one week, a Muslim the next or a Rastafarian the following week. Whoever (group or individual) is the most convincing at any given time can persuade the Marshmallow Man to negotiate his faith. Marshmallow Men also grow weaker under pressure rather than stronger, unlike men of conviction. Marshmallow Men can't withstand the process of going through the refining furnace, because everyone knows that if you put a marshmallow in a fire, it will shrivel up. God wants men of conviction, not men who are always wavering.

Additional reading: Colossians 3:6-10

Soul Check

Are you a marshmallow man?

Confession

I am a man of conviction, not preference.

Day 14

"Mixed Men"

Romans 1:24-27

Wherefore God also gave them up to uncleanness through the lusts of their own hearts, to dishonour their own bodies between themselves: Who changed the truth of God into a lie, and worshipped and served the creature more than the Creator, who is blessed for ever. Amen. For this cause God gave them up unto vile affections: for even their women did change the natural use into that which is against nature. And likewise also the men, leaving the natural use of the woman, burned in their lust one toward another; men with men working that which is unseemly, and receiving in themselves that recompence of their error which was meet.

The third of kind men that exist in the world today is the "Mixed Men." Now this type of man has a sexual gender identity crisis in his life. Men like this think the Bible says "Adam and Steve" instead of Adam and Eve." The devotion for the day is by no means an attempt to judge or criticize any homosexual, but only to share the truth from God's perspective. I fully understand from conversations with homosexuals that some of them chose that particular lifestyle due to sexual abuse when they were children, or from having effeminate tendencies and adapting that type of learned behavior. I don't negate the reasons for why they have that type of behavior. However, I have a serious problem with those who claim that they were born that way. I share with them that the solution to their problem is easy; all they have to do is be "born again." (John 3:3-8) Not only do "Mixed Men" need to be "born again," but so do "Macho Men" and "Marshmallow Men." God is waiting for us to acknowledge what type of man we are so that He can transform us into the man that He desires us to be, a Mighty Man of God!

Additional reading: 1 Corinthians 6:9-11, John 3:3-8

Soul Check

Are you a mixed man?

Confession

I am who God created me to be when He placed me in my mother's womb and He chose my gender. There is no more confusion because I am born again.

Day 15

"Mighty Men"

Joel 3:9

Proclaim ye this among the Gentiles; Prepare war, wake up the mighty men, let all the men of war draw near; let them come up.

The fourth type of men in the world is the "Mighty Men." Now the "Mighty Man" is a man of conviction and cannot be negotiated out of his faith. Like the Apostle Paul, he is persuaded in the One in whom he believes. He also grows stronger under pressure, not weaker. A Mighty Man of God also continues to strive to be like Jesus, knowing that Christlikeness and manhood are synonymous. To be like Christ, one must adapt and adhere to the three main characteristics that Jesus possessed:

1) He must be <u>submitted</u>, remembering that Christ said, "Father, not my will, but Your will be done." (Luke 22:42)

2) He must be <u>consistent</u> just as the Lord was consistent. The Bible says, "He is the same yesterday, today and tomorrow." (Hebrews 13:8)

3) He must have the same characteristic that Jesus had as the cornerstone of His character, which is <u>faithfulness</u>. (Revelation 1:5)

God wants to "wake up the Mighty Men" so that He can pour out His Spirit upon them and bring about complete restoration in their lives. Having learned about the four kinds of men in the world, isn't it time for you to decide what type of man you want to be and need to be?

Additional reading: 2 Timothy 1:12, Joel 2:28

Soul Check

Are you submitted, consistent and faithful?

Confession

I am a mighty man of God because I am submitted, consistent, and faithful.

Day 16

"It's All Good"

Romans 8:28

And we know that all things work together for good to them that love God, to them who are the called according to his purpose.

A popular cliché among the older generation, as well as the new generation when things or situations are okay or not, is "it's all good." Many don't realize the truth to that saying, mainly because it has been so perverted. They don't see or acknowledge God working in all things for the good ... The expression, "it's all good," is often used to cover up some hurt or failed expectation. I really began to notice that when a lot of inmates return from court after having received a negative report. They pretend that it doesn't bother them, but you can see it all over their face and hear it in their voices when they claim "it's all good". If only they knew the truth to that statement when God is in control. When Jesus is the head of their lives, with the revelation of God working in all things (legal or otherwise) for the good of those who love Him and are called according to His purpose, they will understand that it is indeed all good. He turns negative into positive, and the unclean He cleans, He takes that which is crooked and makes it straight. Yes, He will take you from the guttermost to the uttermost, all for his transcendent glory, proving that it's all good.

Soul Check

Is it "all good"?

Confession

I love God, and I am called according to His purpose; therefore, all things will work for my good.

Day 17

"Angry Young Men"

Ephesians 4:26-27

Be ye angry, and sin not: let not the sun goes down upon your wrath: Neither give place to the devil.

Preparing for today's devotion, I had to turn my attention to the younger generation that fills our prison system to get their opinion of why are they so angry? I know that we all get angry at times, and even Jesus got angry when He threw the moneychangers out of the temple. Anger isn't a sin as many suppose; otherwise, Jesus wouldn't have been angry. No, anger is amoral and only becomes sin when we let it get out of control. Webster's dictionary defines anger as: *a strong feeling of displeasure.* Some synonyms are: irate, mad, wrath or upset, all of which can lead to sin when it's out of control. The Bible tells us "to be angry but sin not." A classic case of anger out of control was Cain when he killed his brother Abel, and for what? Because God accepted Abel's offering! When I inquired about why so many young men were angry, most responded because they feel nobody likes them or is on their side. Over half actually said they didn't know but felt that it had a lot to do with their upbringing and hatred for their fathers deserting them. They felt that because they weren't loved and cared for by their father, then they don't love or care about anybody. What a sad commentary for the older generation. Thank God, there is an answer to this dilemma.

Additional reading: Mark 11:15-17, Genesis 4:5-8

Soul Check

Are you angry or have anger hidden in your heart?

Confession

I will not remain angry and give place to the devil.

Day 18

"Temporarily Disconnected"

Psalm 73:2-3, 17

But as for me, my feet were almost gone: my steps had well nigh slipped. For I was envious at the foolish, when I saw the prosperity of the wicked ... until I went into the sanctuary of God; then understood I their end.

The psalmist declares that his feet had almost slipped when he had become envious of the prosperity of the evildoers. As a result, he became "temporarily disconnected." He had taken his focus off of his priestly duties and started looking at the prosperity of the wicked. He got distracted, and his distraction led to being "temporarily disconnected." He actually became envious of evildoers until he began to question his service to God. Many of those in jails and prisons have experienced the same plight as Asaph did, which has resulted in their backslidden condition. They want to come back, but most don't know how. Asaph's experience gives us some insight into how he regained his focus and then became connected to his source again. Verse 17 says that "... I went into the sanctuary of God, then I understood their end." Once you return to the sanctuary of God and reconnect to the source of all life, then you can get out of a backslidden condition. Thank God, we aren't "permanently disconnected." Knowing the end result of the wicked should motivate us to stay focused and pray for those who are temporarily disconnected.

Additional reading: Psalm 73:1-20

Soul Check

Are you temporarily disconnected?

Confession

I will stay connected and worship daily in the sanctuary of God!

Day 19

"Fatherlessness"

Psalm 68:5

A father of the fatherless, and a judge of the widows, is God in his holy habitation.

After reading yesterday's devotion about the comments made by young men in reference to their fathers, I felt compelled to address that issue in today's devotion. During the Sixties and Seventies, we experienced what Dr. Edwin Louis Cole termed "The Absentee Father." Many men were absentee fathers in the sense that they were absent from the home physically but did supply monetary support for their family. However, in the Nineties, the condition within our society has escalated into a state of "fatherlessness." Fatherlessness is more severe than the absentee father in that there isn't any concern at all for the family. Most men and women in the penal system never had a father in the home, so they can't relate to a heavenly Father. So when it comes to "fatherhood," most guys don't have a clue; thus we have the greatest vacuum mankind has ever had in this area. Remember, God is the "father to the fatherless". God has always had a heart for the fatherless and now wants to restore the role of fatherhood in the lives of those who may have been victims of this crazy state of "fatherlessness." He's writing to teach us how to be real fathers, both physically and spiritually, to this "fatherless" generation. Hallelujah!

Additional reading: Psalm 82:3, Psalm 10:14, 18, James 1:27

Soul Check

Are you missing in action? Are you an absentee father?

Confession

I will break the generational curse of fatherlessness and I will not be an absentee father. Teach me, Holy Spirit, how to restore my relationships with my children.

Day 20

"U Got Mail"

Romans 12:2

And be not conformed to this world: but be ye transformed by the renewing of your mind that ye may prove what is that good, and acceptable, and perfect, will of God.

In today's highly technical society, we have computerized just about everything that can be computerized: our cars, phone systems, household appliances, as well as our desk and laptop computers. The technology has gotten so advanced that almost everything that is computerized has voice recognition so you don't have to do anything to operate it other than speak to it. One of the features that has always sparked my interest was the "U Got Mail" feature. Though a simple feature compared to the many functions most computerized gadgets have, it lets you know that someone wants to communicate with you. When that icon pops up, it grabs your attention, and you're quick to check out that email as soon as possible. Well, long before we had all of these advanced means of communication, God was trying to tell us that "U Got Mail" via the Bible. The Bible is God's letter to us and one of His primary means of communication with us. We may have advancements in our technology, but they will never take the place of the written communication the Bible has for us. So the next time you see that icon that says "U Got Mail," just remember that Our Heavenly Father has a letter (mail) for us each and every day.

Additional reading: Psalm 68:19

Soul Check

Did you renew your mind today?

Confession

I will daily renew my mind in His Word.

Day 21

"Don't Look Back"

Jeremiah 29:11

For I know the thoughts that I think toward you, saith the Lord, thoughts of peace, and not of evil, to give you an expected end.

I believe that the main variable that has kept many going through the revolving door of our correctional system is their constantly looking back to their past and not ahead to their future. Jesus warns us that we cannot put our hand to the plow and look back … Not only will we continue going through the never-ending revolving door, but we also will find ourselves not fit for Kingdom use. Bishop T.D. Jakes says it best in his quote, "You can't do anything about your past, but you can do something about your future." Another man of God, Dr. A.R. Bernard from Christian Culture Centre in New York, says that "a man who has no vision is destined to repeat his past." I personally believe that to be true, because all vision is revelation about our future which God promised would be good and not evil. Looking back only prolongs and delays us reaching our future and destiny. Lot's wife would have enjoyed a bright future with her husband had she not looked back. Many times we get real comfortable with the familiar, which causes us to want to return to our past. No matter what you are facing in the near future, confront it and know that the outcome will be good and not evil. Believe me, your future looks much brighter than your darkened past. Remember, the past has no power over your future. Praise God!

Additional Reading: Luke 9:62, Genesis 19:17-26

Soul Check

Why do you keep looking back and remembering what happened in the past?

Confession

I will not look back! I am letting go of the past and letting God direct me towards my future.

Day 22

"Isolation = Selfishness"
"Isolation is Selfishness"

Proverbs 18:1a (CEV)

It's selfish and stupid to think only of yourself...

Many people wouldn't automatically consider isolation to be equated with selfishness. But let's consider this same premise from what the Word of God says, and maybe even consider some Biblical examples. Proverbs 18:1a (CEV) says "It is selfish and stupid to think only yourself." The King James Version puts it this way: "A man who isolates himself seeks his own desire." So there is definitely a correlation between isolation and selfishness. This principle doesn't apply to those who are forced into isolation, such as cases in the penal system. Prisoners are put in isolation for protection or punishment. Today's devotion is mainly for those who have voluntarily placed themselves in isolation. Elijah wanted to isolate himself after being threatened by Jezebel. The prophet Jonah sought to isolate himself from his God-given assignment and ended up in the belly of a great fish. These are just a few examples of men of God who sought their own selfish interest through isolation. But the Lord spoke to both of them, just as He will speak to us when we feel the urge to isolate ourselves. Getting alone with God for a season of prayer and fasting isn't the same as isolation. Plus, you aren't alone in those seasons because the Lord is there with you. Praise God!

Additional Reading: 1 Kings 19:4-9, 13, Jonah 1:2-17

Soul Check

Are you a loner? Are you isolating yourself?

Confession

I will not isolate myself but be obedient to what God is calling me to do.

Day 23

"Count the Cost"

Luke 14:28-30

For which of you, intending to build a tower, sitteth not down first, and counteth the cost, whether he have sufficient to finish it? Lest haply, after he had laid the foundation, and is not able to finish it, all that behold it began to mock him, Saying, This man began to build and was not able to finish.

Jesus tells us in the parable of the tower that we must "count the cost" before we start so that we will be able to finish. In today's devotion, I want all of us who have been affected by the correctional system as we know it today, to see if you can pinpoint just when that inmate or former inmate didn't "count the cost." I believe that many just didn't realize just how not "counting the cost" would affect so many people. Usually, the mind-set of the incarcerated individual is, "It only affects me," so there really isn't any reason to count the cost. Oh, how wrong they are! Because they failed to count the cost, many of their families and friends were hurt more than they will ever know. Relationships, emotions, mental capacity and even spiritual growth have been affected and ruined by that individual who failed to count the cost. We not only need to count the cost when we are about to build on some aspect of our life such as employment, home or career, but we especially need to follow the Scriptural advice in Luke 14:28 as it applies to all relationships: First, our relationship with the Lord, and then our relationships with our fellow man must be considered. So before you set out on some new endeavor or start some new relationship, count the cost to make sure that you can finish what you start, and look closely at all the folks that may be affected by what you do.

Additional Reading: Proverbs 24:27, Proverbs 27:23-27

Soul Check

Are you counting the cost?

Confession

I will count the cost and finish what I start.

Day 24

"Handmade by God"

Psalms 139:13-18

For thou hast possessed my reins: thou hast covered me in my mother's womb. I will praise thee; for I am fearfully and wonderfully made: marvelous are thy works; and that my soul knoweth right well. My substance was not hid from thee when I was made in secret, and curiously wrought in the lowest parts of the earth. Thine eyes did see my substance, yet being unperfect; and in thy book all my members were written, which in continuance were fashioned, when as yet there was none of them. How precious also are thy thoughts unto me, O God! How great is the sum of them! If I should count them, they are more in number than the sand: when I awake, I am still with thee.

Low self-esteem and feelings of insecurity are two of the top behavioral patterns displayed in most controlled environments. So much negativity has been perpetrated upon these individuals until it becomes rather difficult to see themselves in any positive role. Well, I have good news for you, my friend; when the Lord made you, He had something so special in mind that none of the five billion people who have lived on this earth in the past, nor the six billion who live- on the planet today have what you have. You were and are so special to God that He finished creating you, He threw the mold away so that nobody else would ever be like you. That's why you are the only one with your fingerprints and the DNA that you have. Even if you are an identical twin, you still are uniquely different. No- wonder the label that the Lord wants us to wear should read, "Handmade by God." Hallelujah! God took His time creating you, and with a very, very special purpose, I might add. The talents, the gifts, the skill, the intellect, the personality and whatever else He knew you would need were carefully and uniquely designed just for you. We wear all kinds of labels on our clothes and other possessions, but the main one we all need to be cognizant of is the one that declares, "Handmade by God!"

Additional Reading: Genesis 1:26-27

Soul Check

Are you an original or an imitator?

Confession

I am fearfully and wonderfully made. I am written in Your book. You are thinking of me.

Day 25

"The Master Plan"

Ephesians 5:17

Wherefore be ye not unwise, but understanding what the will of the Lord is.

As we struggle through life without God's instructions and directions, we tend to let everyone, including ourselves, make life's plan for us. However, being fallible and limited, we often miss the mark and end up living far below the level that God wants us to live. Jeremiah 29:11 clearly lets us know that "He knows what He has planned for us." That plan is for our good, to give us a future and a hope. All of the plans that man and any manmade institutions come up with cannot compare with the plan that God has for us. Ephesians 5:17 in the Message says, "Don't live carelessly, unthinkingly. Make sure you understand what the Master wants." What does He want and what is the ultimate motivation for creating us? Well, Isaiah 43:7 says, "God has created us for His glory." Some may think that they can't glorify the Lord while incarcerated or on probation or parole. Being in a structured environment is one of the easiest places to learn how to glorify Him. It may not be the ideal, but you can learn of the Master's plan for your life. As a matter of fact, He permitted you to be where you are just to show you that all of those other plans weren't working for you. Isn't it time you start to find out what God has planned for you and live accordingly? Pray that He will reveal His plan for your life right now. You won't be disappointed! Selah.

Additional Reading: Jeremiah 29:11, Isaiah 43:7

Soul Check

Are you walking in wisdom and understanding?

Confession

I am wise and have understanding of the will of the Lord for me.

Day 26

"Words Do Hurt"

Proverbs 18:21

Death and life are in the power of the tongue: and they that love it shall eat the fruit thereof.

Growing up, most of us have heard or said the familiar cliché, "Sticks and stones may break my bones, but words will never hurt me." Like everything else the devil touches, this cliché too has been perverted. Because sticks and stones will definitely break your bones when hit hard enough, and words will not only hurt you--words will also kill you. The Bible says "that the power of death and life are in the tongue." We all need to watch what we say, knowing that we either curse or bless an individual by what we say. So many altercations in the jails and prisons could be avoided if only they could learn how to tame their tongues. What's so sad is that we often know just what words to speak to get someone upset and provoke them to respond_ in like manner. I remember my wife telling me years ago that verbal abuse is much more hurtful than physical abuse. Millions of relationships have been destroyed basically as a result of what was spoken out of our mouths. Generations have been cursed based on what was spoken over them. Let's pray that we will speak only blessings over our family and friends. We will even bless those who curse us and break the generational curse. Lord, please help us to watch the words we speak.

Additional Reading: James 3:5-12, Matthew 5:44-45

Soul Check

Do your words build up or tear down?

Confession

I will speak life and not death; blessings and not curses.

Day 27

"Least Likely"

Acts 9:1, 2

And Saul, yet breathing out threatenings and slaughter against the disciples of the Lord, went unto the high priest, and desired of him letters to Damascus to the synagogues, that if he found any of this way, whether they were men or women, he might bring them bound unto Jerusalem.

I suppose that _ of all the Biblical characters, the Apostle Paul, probably was the "least likely" to be saved or used by God. We know today because of the written Word that he was a spiritual giant. He was a missionary, an apostle and Bible writer, as well as a worker of miracles. Yet, because he persecuted the Church, most of his contemporaries felt that as a Pharisee_ he would never be saved. The Scriptures in Acts, Chapter 9 confirm this premise, plus Paul tells us himself in 1 Timothy that he persecuted the Church. Yet in spite of it all, God still could save Paul and use him for His Kingdom. Many individuals that have had some sort of run-in with the law or have become victims of neo-type slavery system feel that they are the "least likely" to be saved or used by God! Those who know them or have had some association with them feel the same as Paul's contemporaries felt about him. Even some of their family members feel that way about them, and nothing can change their minds. However, there is a God who says "... before I placed you in your mother's womb, I knew you." (Jeremiah 1:5) So remember that you are not the "least likely" to be saved and used by God, but rather you are destined for greatness. What God has made you overcomes what the world has made you. So walk in your greatness now!

Additional Reading: 1 Timothy 1:13, Acts 9:10-16

Soul Check

Do you feel your are the least likely to be saved and used by God?

Confession

I am destined for greatness.

Day 28

"A.A." (Attitude Adjustment)

Romans 12: 1, 2

I beseech you therefore, brethren, by the mercies of God, that ye present your bodies a living sacrifice, holy, acceptable unto God, which is your reasonable service. And be not conformed to this world: but be ye transformed by the renewing of your mind, that ye may prove what is that good, and acceptable, and perfect, will of God.

I know that the first thing that come to most people minds when they see "A.A." is Alcoholics Anonymous. Yet, that isn't the meaning _or the topic of today's devotion. What "A.A" stands for in our devotion for today is "Attitude Adjustment," because a lot of us really need one. Merriam Webster dictionary defines attitude as: 1) posture; 2) a mental position or feeling with regard to a fact or state; 3) the position of something in relation to something else; 4) a negative or hostile state of mind and 5) a cocky or arrogant manner. Though all five definitions are applicable pertaining to attitude adjustment, I would like for us to look at the latter two, because what makes our attitude unacceptable to God and to one another is the negative, hostile, cocky and arrogant manner we display. Nobody likes someone who always has an attitude problem. We are going to look at several different attitudes in this book, but first let's see how we can adjust our attitude. According to today's Scripture, we adjust our attitude by renewing our minds. It won't happen overnight since it is harder to unlearn something than it is to learn something new. Yet, with the help of the Holy Spirit and God's grace, we can do it. We have the victory. Thank you Jesus!

Additional Reading: 1 John 2:15, Ephesians 4:23, 1 Thessalonians 4:1-12

Soul Check

Are you in need of an attitude adjustment?

Confession

I will renew my mind so that my attitude will be adjusted to the perfect will of God.

Day 29

"Forget the Past"

Isaiah 43:18, 19

Remember ye not the former things neither consider the things of old. Behold, I will do a new thing; now it shall spring forth; shall ye not know it? I will even make a way in the wilderness, and rivers in the desert.

Because the past has played such a dominant role in the shaping of our present, I want to share on this topic several times in this devotional book. So many individuals are imprisoned by their past until it is almost impossible to live in the present, let alone make plans for the future. Contrary to popular opinion, experience isn't always the best teacher unless you have learned from that experience. It makes no difference whether you've been in a correctional facility or not--if you haven't learned something from your negative experiences from the past, you will be prone to repeat them and consequently remain a victim of your past. How do I get out, you may ask? Well, the Bible gives us the clear-cut answer in Isaiah 43:18 when it declares, "Do not remember the former (past) things, nor consider the things of old". I also like the way the Apostle Paul warns us, " ... forgetting those things which are behind ..." Yes, saints, whether you are behind the walls reading this or a relative of someone who is a victim of this penal system, remember that the past may have influenced and shaped our present, but it doesn't have to have anything to do with our future. I decree that you are hereby set free from the past that has kept you imprisoned for so many years, in the name of Jesus!

Additional Reading: Philippians 3:13, 14; Luke 9:62

Soul Check

Why are you holding on to the past?

Confession

I am forgetting the past and will not allow it to dictate my present or future.

Day 30

"Be Content"

2 Corinthians 4:16-18

For which cause we faint not; but though our outward man perish, yet the inward man is renewed day by day. For our light affliction, which is but for a moment, worketh for us a far more exceeding and eternal weight of glory;

Living in a society that is highly based on material things and the acquiring of them, it becomes rather difficult to be content with what we have. Yet, we must remember that the things which are seen are only temporary. I've personally learned that "keeping up with the Jones" isn't where it's at. 1 Timothy 6:8 says, "Having food and clothing, be content with these." Striving to be rich in this world produces greed and avarice. Who we are and what God has planned for us to become isn't predicated on what we have. Don't get me wrong, it's okay to be rich and even acquire wealth. But when it gets to the point where we will do anything or ruin anybody to get these riches, then I suggest as the Apostle Paul did, that no matter what state we are in, we can learn to be content. Many lives have been lost, and many years have been wasted away behind bars as a result of not knowing how to be content with what we have. I think Jesus says it best when He encourages us to "store up treasures in heaven where rust and moth can't destroy them nor thieves can break in and steal them." Now that sounds like being content with what you have while simultaneously laying up treasures in heaven. Praise God!

Additional Reading: Hebrews 13:5; Philippians 4:11-13; 1 Timothy 6:8; Matthew 6:19-21

Soul Check

Are you content?

Confession

I am learning to be content with what I have.

Day 31

"Spiritual Tune Up"

1 Thessalonians 5:15-24

See that none render evil for evil unto any man; but ever follow that which is good, both among ourselves, and to all men. Rejoice evermore. Pray without ceasing. In everything give thanks: for this is the will of God in Christ Jesus concerning you. Quench not the Spirit. Despise not prophesying. Prove all things; hold fast that which is good. Abstain from all appearance of evil. And the very God of peace sanctify you wholly; and I pray God your whole spirit and soul and body be preserved blameless unto the coming of our Lord Jesus Christ.

You know, sometimes our everyday Christian walk can become so routine or mundane that we actually could use a "spiritual tune-up." It's sort of similar to giving your car a tune-up. It's not that there is something major wrong with the car, it just needs to be tuned after being driven for so many miles. It just doesn't have the spark or pick-up that it once had. Yeah, it is running a little slow and even misfiring sometimes. But once you change those spark plugs, redo the wiring and reset the timing, everything seems to run like new. Well, just imagine how much more complex we are than cars and how we often feel a little run down. Well, we're okay in that we are still striving to walk uprightly in our integrity. We just feel a little sluggish. Well, it's nothing a spiritual tune-up won't take care of. Maybe a review of some of our spiritual disciplines and a self-inventory will lead us to do a "spiritual tune-up" on ourselves. Some examples of spiritual disciplines are: 1) prayer time 2) daily devotion 3) fasting or 4) keeping a journal. Maybe we've become sluggish in one or more of these areas, and we want to fine-tune our spiritual engine (heart), then get a "spiritual tune up"!

Additional Reading: Jude 20; Matthew 17:21; Habakkuk 2:2,3

Soul Check

Is your spirit out of tune?

Confession

It's time to fine-tune my spirit. I am getting a spiritual tune-up!

Day 32

Real Maturity

Luke 12:48

But he that knew not, and did commit things worthy of stripes, shall be beaten with few stripes. For unto whomsoever much is given, of him shall be much required: and to whom men have committed much, of him they will ask the more.

A great man of the modern-day men's movement, Dr. Edwin Louis Cole, shared a principle that remains as crystal clear today as the first time I heard it. That principle is that "real maturity doesn't come with age but with the acceptance of responsibility." That's why some men seventeen years of age are more mature then some men who are forty-seven--because they accepted responsibility, and the older men didn't. Our jails and our prisons are full up with what I call "adult adolescents." They have failed to accept responsibility both on the outside and on the inside, so they never really reach the level of maturity that the Lord desires for them to have. The principle can be seen in Luke 12:48. It was the Hebrew custom that a Hebrew male receive responsibility (religious) at about thirteen years of age. If he passed his bar mitzvah, he then entered into manhood. God wants us to grow up and not stay infants or spiritual babes, and that growing-up process begins and ends with accepting responsibility. To get "real maturity," especially in your spiritual walk, I encourage you to read and study Romans 12 and 13. Begin by accepting responsibility for your actions, and pray for the Holy Spirit to help you.

Additional Reading: 2 Peter 3:18; Romans 12; Romans 13

Soul Check

Are you accepting responsibility for your actions?

Confession

I am accepting responsibility for my actions.

Day 33

"Rules of Engagement"

Job 1 and 2

I remember sharing a message titled, "What to do when all hell breaks loose" with the men in a correctional facility. The context of the message focused on the unwarranted suffering of Job. Though Job was an upright man and shunned evil, God still allowed him to suffer. Yet, in all of his suffering, Job never cursed or blamed God for His situation. Instead of complaining, he chose to follow the "rules of engagement," which consist of the following acronym: R.U.L.E.S.

"R" is for recognizing that you are going through a process that will be necessary for your growth.

"U" is for understanding that you must go through the process, nobody else can do it for you, nor can you run or hide from the process. You must go through it.

"L" is for learning from the process. Once you learn from the process you can benefit from it.

"E" is for enduring the process. No matter how difficult it was, Job trusted God and endured it.

"S" is for successfully going through the process and entering the restoration stage.

So no matter how difficult the process or trial may seem, just follow the "RULES" of engagement. Lord, thank you for the strength to endure the process.

Additional Reading: Job 42:10-13

Soul Check

Are you following the rules of engagement?

Confession

I will follow the "RULES of engagement."

Day 34

"Going in Circles"

Numbers 14

Sometimes I think about how the Israelites kept wandering around the wilderness, going in circles because of the rebelliousness and their disobedience. I often compare it to the lifestyles of those who are incarcerated and don't have freedom of movement. Their lives become constant mundane, routine and vacuous "going in circles." They want to make some progress and enter into their spiritual promise land, but they are stuck in a cycle of sinning, repenting, and confessing. Because the environment in which they live is 90% negative and they are still babes in Christ, they often repeat the cycle and end up "going in circles," around and around just like in the wilderness. However, the good news is that they can break the cycle simply by trusting God to deliver them and knowing that He will never leave or forsake them. Don't become like the Israelites who were afraid to confront the giants and the obstacles in their lives, because if you do, you'll end up wasting valuable time "going in circles." Once you decide to break the pattern, the Lord will assist you in overcoming and walking in total victory, even in prison. We are more than conquerors. Praise God!

Additional Reading: Hebrews 13:5; Romans 8:37

Soul Check

Are you going in circles?

Confession

I will no longer go in circles. I am breaking the pattern.

Day 35

"Don't Get It Twisted"

1 Samuel Chapter 1

One thing I've learned from being in a structured, controlled environment is that those who make up this population are great storytellers. Not only that, but they love to have stories told to them. Well, following the theme from today's devotion, I want to share a brief story with you about someone who really got it twisted. His name is Goliath, and he taunted the men of Israel who where afraid of him. Yet David, when he heard the taunts, went to King Saul and assured him that he would kill Goliath. I can just imagine this young ruddy-looking boy standing there challenging this great big giant, saying, "Don't get it twisted." (Don't get it wrong). Goliath may have been confident in his size, strength and his champion reputation, but he truly had it all wrong. Not everyone was in fear of him, so when David showed up to fight, Goliath said, "Am I a dog that you come to me with sticks?" Then after he had cursed David and his God, David let him know that he got it all "twisted," and that he would be delivered into his hands and he would have his head. The Lord expects us to walk in truth and righteousness just like David, so let's check out the stories we tell and whatever we do, "Don't get it twisted."

Additional Reading: 1 Samuel 17:43-45

Soul Check

Are you twisted?

Confession

I won't get it twisted!

Day 36

Get Wisdom

Proverbs 4:7

"Wisdom is the principle thing; therefore get wisdom: and with all thy getting get understanding."

Most men and women who have been in or are in some sort of correctional facility always pride themselves on how much they know. I mean that they will argue about anything from animals to aerodynamics, from music to monsters and definitely from preachers to politics. And the amazing thing is that they are wrong about 95 per cent of the time. True, they do have some knowledge, but it is so misguided. They need to learn that "wisdom" is more important than just mere knowledge or even understanding. Knowledge is the acquiring of facts or the truth of something learned, whereas understanding is the interpreting of the facts or the truth learned. Yet, wisdom is the application of the facts and the truth learned. Having knowledge without wisdom is just like having a bar of soap and not using it; you still stay dirty. The Bible says that wisdom is the principle thing, so get wisdom. Don't get it wrong--you do need knowledge and understanding just as much as you need wisdom. They all work together. My prayer is that you don't just attain a lot of knowledge or understanding at the expense of wisdom, for then you would only have head knowledge and not wisdom of the heart. May the Lord bless you with the wisdom that is from above.

Additional Reading: Proverbs 8:1-36; Proverbs 5:1-3; James 1:5, 3:17

Soul Check

Are you seeking wisdom and understanding from above?

Confession

I will seek wisdom and obtain understanding from above.

Day 37

We Are the Greatest

John 14:12

"Verily, verily, I say unto you, he that believeth on me, the works that I do shall he do also; and greater works than these shall he do; because I go unto my Father."

When I was a young man growing up in Brooklyn, New York, boxing was a must if you were to survive in the streets, juvenile facilities or youth homes. It's as if we all had a chip on our shoulder, rebelled against authority or just wanted to prove that we were the toughest and the greatest with our hands. One of our contemporary professional boxers was Muhammad Ali, who some say till this day that "he was the greatest heavyweight of all time." Well, that may ring true for many in boxing circles today, at least until someone else comes along. However, I can prove to you that spiritually we who are in Christ are the "greatest of all time." For the Spirit of God that dwells in us makes us greater than any man-made institution or agency that ever existed. 1 John 4:4 says, "Greater is He that is in you than he who is in the world." Jesus confirms this with His declaration that "greater works we would do ..." (*paraphrase mine*) John 14:12. So when we look at ourselves from God's perspective through Jesus, we are indeed "the greatest." But don't get puffed up; stay humble, remembering that He also said. "The greatest among you would be a servant of all." Mark 9:34-35. Plus, you must be childlike in order to enter the kingdom of God.

Additional Reading: Matthew 11:11, 1 John 4:4, Matthew 18:1-4

Soul Check

Are you being a servant?

Confession

I believe on Him, and being a servant, I shall do greater works.

Day 38

Stop Whaling

Ephesians 4:25

"Wherefore putting away lying, speak every man truth with his neighbour: for we are members one of another."

When I first heard the term, "stop whaling," I thought that it referred to some type of movement to stop killing or harming whales. Why, just last year when I went to Hawaii (Maui), I found it real fascinating because it was "whale season," and whale watching was highly recommended. My wife and I went, and it was interesting, to say the least. It wasn't until I talked to a few of the guys at the correctional facility that I mustered up enough nerve to ask them what it meant. The slang, "stop whaling," actually means to "stop lying" or "stretching the truth." Having done a lot of fishing and told quite a few fish stories, I found out that "whaling" is the biggest fish stories or lies one can tell. So when someone is caught telling a huge fish story or lie, they will tell that individual to "stop whaling." Well, the Bible commands us to "... put away lying ..." Colossians 3:9 tells us, "Do not lie to one another, since you have put off the old man with his deeds." Plus, even though many don't take lying as serious as some sins such as murder, adultery or stealing, God takes it very seriously. As a matter of fact, He calls it an abomination and lists lying as number two on the list of seven things God hates the most. We will definitely do another devotion on this topic but for now, remember the next time you hear "stop whaling," you'll know it means "stop lying."

Additional Reading: Colossians 3:9; Proverbs 6:17

Soul Check

Are you whaling?

Confession

I will stop whaling and tell the truth.

Day 39

"I" Trouble

Revelation 3:18

"I counsel thee to buy of me gold tried in the fire, that thou mayest be rich; and white raiment that thou mayest be clothed, and that the shame of thy nakedness do not appear; and anoint thine eyes with eyesalve, that thou mayest see."

As I was writing another devotion dealing with sin, I couldn't shake the thoughts that are featured in today's devotion. When I began to look at the sins we commit on a daily basis, I couldn't help but conclude that we all have "I" trouble," not in an optical sense, but in a selfish sense. For the "me, myself and I" syndrome is always the dominate factor when we sin. As a matter of fact the core of sin is "I." Yes, we were born with sin, and even have become victims of generational curses that influence us to sin. But regardless of whether our sin is intentional or unintentional, whether it is inherited or not, most of the time we are definitely at the center of it. Ask the Holy Spirit to show you where you are the focal point of your sinning; then repent for your sins, confessing them out of your life. With the "I" trouble we have, only a spiritual eye salve will heal us. When we take the "I" from the core of sin, then we can let Jesus be the center of our lives. Thank the Lord for reminding us that we all have or have had "I" trouble at some time in our life, but we can be delivered when we walk in obedience and let God be God. O how I love Him, O how He loves me.

Additional Reading: Philippians 2:3; Galatians 5:26; Romans 2:10

Soul Check

Do you have "I" trouble?

Confession

Lord, let me see where I have "I" trouble.

Day 40

Dare to Be Different (Part I – Chosen Generation)

1 Peter 2:9

"But ye are a chosen generation, a royal priesthood, a holy nation, a peculiar people; that ye should shew forth the praises of him who hath called you out of darkness into his marvelous light."

Many from my generation would dare to label the next generation the X-generation-- the X being a symbol that denotes the unknown. So what we are really saying to our children and grandchildren is that their generation is a generation of the unknown (X). However, that's not who God says they are. As a matter of fac, He calls them "… a chosen generation, a royal priesthood, a holy nation, a peculiar people, that you may proclaim the praises of Him who called you out of darkness into His marvelous light." (1 Peter 2:9). If you pay real close attention to this Scripture, you will notice that it says nothing about being an "X" (unknown) generation. As a matter of fact, God says just the opposite. He calls you a "chosen generation," meaning that He knew when He would birth this generation on this earthly scene. He knew the group of people that would make up this generation before the foundation of the world. *Chosen* means that you weren't voted into this generation but rather were selected, handpicked with favoritism, no doubt. So that means you are a special generation. So no matter where you are right now--jail, prison, work camp, or any other correctional facility, don't let nobody label you other than what God has labeled you--"a chosen generation." You are now part of a generation of believers who will usher us into a spiritual promised land. Glory to God!

Additional Reading: Psalm 135:4; John 15:16

Soul Check

Do you know that you have been chosen? Do you know that you are alive now because He ordained this time of your existence and placed you in this generation? What's your purpose?

Confession

Lord, thank you for choosing me for this generation.

Day 41

Dare to Be Different (Part II - Royal Priesthood)

1 Peter 2:9

But ye are a chosen generation, a royal priesthood, an holy nation, a peculiar people; that ye should shew forth the praises of him who hath called you out of darkness into his marvelous light ...

Do you sometimes feel like people have labeled you according to your behavior (what you do or have done) and not according to who God says you are (the real you)? Well, if you've said "yes," let me encourage you to stop looking at yourself based on who others say you are. It doesn't matter whether you've been arrested before, locked up before or have had any contact with our judicial or penal system. You're not who they say you are. Remember God made you different from every other creation and called you "a chosen generation" and then "a royal priesthood." What--Royal as in kingly or regal? Yes, you became a person of royal blood when you accepted Jesus as your Lord and Saviour. Then, to make you the cream of the crop, He decided that you would be a "royal priesthood," meaning that not only are you kingly, but you are a king-priest after the order of Melchizedek! Yes, this order (Melchizedek) is a higher order of priesthood because it includes being both king and priest. Kings are those who govern, whereas priests are those who hear from the people and petition God on their behalf. So recognize who you are in God's household and in his scheme of things. Does this sound like an unknown generation? I think not – Yet, He doesn't finish there. Check out tomorrow's devotion!

Additional reading: Hebrew 7:17, 21; Psalm 110:4

Soul Check

Do you recognize the king in you? Do you realize that you are royalty?

Confession

I am a king and have inherited a royal kingdom.

Day 42

Dare to Be Different (Part 3 – A Holy Nation)

1 Peter 2:9

But ye are a chosen generation, a royal priesthood, an holy nation, a peculiar people; that ye should shew forth the praises of him hath called you out of darkness into his marvelous light ....

Continuing on in the same spirit as the last two days of devotions, let's recap: God says we are "a chosen generation", "a royal priesthood". Then He continues on calling us "a holy nation." Now, considering most of our past and the run-ins we had with the law and our experience with drugs and alcohol, the last thing we would call ourselves is "Holy." Well, thank God that He is the one describing us and not we ourselves. He's not calling us all of this because of us, but because of what Jesus has done (Hallelujah). A "Holy Nation"-- what does that entail? Well, let's start with the word *nation*. God never deals with races of people in the Bible, but only with nations, and He declares that out of one man He made all the nations of the earth. *Holy* means that we have been set apart by God and for God's own special use. Synonyms for Holy are separate, sanctified, consecrated, hallowed or blessed. The sacred connotation reveals just how special we are to God when we join the elite group of saints. Yes, your entire Christian walk will be predicated upon your identity in Christ. Know who you are, man of God, woman of God, and don't let anybody tell you different. You are a chosen generation, a royal priesthood, a holy nation and a peculiar people.

Additional reading: Exodus 19:6; Acts 17:26

Soul Check

Are you holy? If no, why not? What is your special use?

Confession

I am holy because I have been set apart by God.

Day 43

Dare to Be Different (Part 4 – Peculiar People)

1 Peter 2:9

But ye are a chosen generation, a royal priesthood, an holy nation, a peculiar people; that ye should shew forth the praises of him hath called you out of darkness into his marvelous light ….

Finally, the Lord declares us to be a peculiar people. Now, in the Old Testament, to be a peculiar people meant to be God's very own special possession or property, a special treasure. God wanted a special people where His Spirit could dwell that would be different then the rest of the nations around them. He didn't want them to be the same as those other pagan nations. That's why in the New Testament the term *peculiar people* meant to be different, strange, odd, distinctive, or weird. You see, the Lord never wanted us to be like everyone else. He created us uniquely different even in an age where everyone strives to be the same. We need to dare to be different. God doesn't want us to adapt the characteristics of the world, nor does He want us to become institutionalized, but to conform to the image of His Son who truly was different. Imagine someone showing up on the scene walking on water, multiplying loaves of bread and fishes, turning water into wine, healing the sick, raising the dead and then ascending back into heaven. Now if that's not strange and daring to be different, I don't know what is. You too can dare to be different right where you are at physically, emotionally, mentally and spiritually because of your identity in Christ. You're a chosen generation, a royal priesthood, a holy nation and a peculiar people.

Additional reading: Deuteronomy 14:2; Deuteronomy 26:18

Soul Check

Are you a peculiar person? What makes you different? Have you identified your God-given treasure?

Confession

I will dare to be different.

Day 44

No Worries

Matthew 6:25-34

When I was in Australia, I noticed that anytime someone wanted to say "Everything is okay," they would say, "No worries." Each time a question was asked, they would always reply, "No worries." I heard that term so much until I actually started to worry. What really tripped me out was when I heard the native aborigines say it. After doing over thirty school assemblies, a dozen or so church services, several men's events and a half a dozen concerts with my son and his group, I finally had the confidence to let them take care of all the details, whether it was in Sydney, Melbourne, Brisbane or Adelaide. Being in that country for over six weeks, I was prone to want to take care of every detail myself. Yet, they convinced me that I had "no worries" and caused me to know through the people of Australia that although I was 10,000 miles away from home, I had "no worries." Even visiting the jails and prisons that are totally different from the system over here, I still had "no worries." So my word of encouragement for you who tend to worry like I used to – is to follow the advice in Matthew 6:33 and remember my friends from the outback country whose favorite saying is "No worries."

Additional reading: Philippians 4:6; Luke 12:29-32

Soul Check

What are you worrying about today? Can you trust God with it? Can you say, I have "no worries!" If no, why not?

Confession

I will not worry but place my trust in Him.

Day 45

Five Major Sins

1 Corinthians 10:6-9

Now these things were our examples, to the intent we should not lust after evil things, as they also lusted. Neither be ye idolaters, as were some of them; as it is written, The people sat down to eat and drink, and rose up to play. Neither let us commit fornication, as some of them committed, and fell in one day three and twenty thousand. Neither let us tempt Christ, as some of them also tempted, and were destroyed of serpents.

The next series of devotions that we will be studying describes the five major sins that kept the children of Israel out of their Canaan land. Now, Canaan land represented a place of abundance, of potential, of fullness, of blessings, a place of maximizing your entire life. The Lord had brought the children of Israel out of Egypt (a place of bondage) and desired to take them right into Canaan land. But because of their complaining and rebelliousness and the five major sins that we will be studying, they ended up in the wilderness (a place of wandering). From Egypt to Canaan land was actually a three-day trip that took them forty years to make, with one generation dying off in the wilderness. Canaan land also symbolizes mankind's maximum potential. God wanted them to trust Him to fulfill His promise to give them the land He swore to their forefathers. Yet, because of the giants (obstacles, major sins) they refused to enter in and subsequently lived far below the level God had planned for them. Many incarcerated individuals and their families haven't entered their Canaan land in their jobs, their marriages, their finances, with their children, or in their manhood or womanhood because of the same five reasons or sins. The Lord wants us to live life to its fullest potential (abundant life). As we continue, we will examine these five major sins so that they won't keep us out of our Canaan land.

Additional reading: Deuteronomy 8:7-10, Deuteronomy 6:10-11; Genesis 17:8

Soul Check

I will examine myself to see if I am living to the fullest potential that God has planned for my life. Have I entered into my Canaan land? If not, why not?

Confession

I will live to the fullest potential that God has planned for me.

Day 46

"Major Sin #1 (Lusting After Evil Things)

James 1:14-15

But every man is tempted, when he is drawn away of his own lust, and enticed. Then when lust hath conceived, it bringeth forth sin: and sin, when it is finished, bringeth forth death.

The first major sin we will look at is "lusting after evil things." This sin will definitely keep you from reaching your Canaan land, because it is a totally selfish one. Lusting after evil things is a desire to please self at the expense of God and others. Evil things extend beyond just the material things. For instance, due to limited movement in a correctional facility, women and drugs are a rarity, so men lust after these things. There is a constant preoccupation with what self wants. Lust is the opposite of love (morally), because it desires to get whereas love desires to give! "Lusting after evil things" is also equated with satisfying or gratifying the flesh. Whatever the flesh wants, lust will accommodate it. The lust we are discussing here has nothing to do with sex, We will look at that in "Major Sin #3." The children of Israel lusted after the things that had been left behind in Egypt. Most of the time inmates spend in prisons or jails is preoccupied with "lusting after evil things" they left on the outside. However, incarceration can be turned into a positive when individuals will use that time to discipline themselves in the Word of God. Then their lust can be converted to love, and they can start experiencing a Canaan land life in prison. The Lord will help to make it possible. Selah.

Additional Reading: James 4:1-3; Romans 13:14; Numbers 11:4; 1 John 2:16-17

Soul Check

Are you lusting after evil things?

Confession

I will not lust after evil things.

Day 47

"Major Sin #2" (Idolatry)

Exodus 32: 4, 6

And he received them at their hand, and fashioned it with a graving tool, after he had made it a molten calf: and they said, These be thy gods, O Israel, which brought thee up out of the land of Egypt ... And they rose up early on the morrow, and offered burnt offerings, and brought peace offerings; and the people sat down to eat and to drink, and rose up to play.

Once we become aware of the definition of idolatry, we can then examine ourselves to see if there are any idols in our lives. Idolatry is a value system we create in which we esteem something or someone to be more worthy of our devotion then God. In our society, some of the more common examples of idolatry are prestige, popularity, money, business, our mates and even our ministries. In an institutional setting where much of the inmates' desires are limited and /or prohibited, they substitute and make idols of other things. Some of their idols are television, cards, rap music, pornography, habitual masturbation, illicit drugs and gambling, to name a few. I believe that the same spirit that exists behind many of society's social and religious ills (idols) is the same spirit that exists behind the value system set up by those who are incarcerated. But the good news is that we can get rid of the idols in our lives, just like the church on the outside can be cleansed of its ills. Jesus is no respecter of persons and desires to see us set free from all idolatry. (1 John 5:21) 1 Corinthians 6:9 tells us that "... idolaters will not inherit the Kingdom of God"! So let's examine ourselves and pray that the Holy Spirit will help us rid ourselves of all idols, so that this sin won't keep us from entering our personal Canaan land!

Additional Reading: Deuteronomy 5:8-9; Romans 1:21, 23; Ezekiel 14: 3-5; 1 Corinthians 6:9

Soul Check

What are your idols?

Confession

I will set no idols before me.

Day 48

"Major Sin #3" (Fornication)

1 Corinthian 10:6-9

Now these things were our examples, to the intent we should not lust after evil things, as they also lusted. Neither be ye idolaters, as were some of them; as it is written. The people sat down to eat and drink, and rose up to play. Neither let us commit fornication, as some of them committed, and fell in one day three and twenty thousand. Neither let us tempt Christ, as some of them also tempted, and were destroyed of serpents.

Dr. Edwin Louis Cole in his book "Maximized Manhood" warned us that sex sins would be the church's' problem today. Well, the prophetic word couldn't have been more timely and accurate than when it was said over twenty years ago. Fornication includes every kind of sex sins. Plus, fornication is nothing new to mankind; it has prevailed since the beginning of time. Sometimes it became so prevalent that God had to destroy whole cities, such as Sodom and Gomorrah. Even when Balaam didn't succeed in cursing the children of Israel for King Balak, he turned to harlotry and got the people to curse themselves. In today's society fornication prevails in the hearts of men like never before. Not only has it increased in its depravity but technology has made it more readily accessible than ever before. Whether one is literally in prison indulging in any sex sin from habitual masturbation to homosexuality, or whether he is mentally and psychologically imprisoned on the outside, it's still a major sin that keeps one from entering the Canaan land. Thank God for the blood of Jesus that isn't selective in the sins He will deliver us from. We already have the victory, so let's walk in it and follow the Biblical admonish to "flee sexual immorality ..." (1 Corinthians 6:18) Praise God!

Additional Reading: 1 Corinthians 6:9, 10; Numbers 25:1-4; Genesis 19; Judges 16:4-21

Soul Check

Are you fornicating?

Confession

I will not break the laws of God by committing fornication.

Day 49

"Major Sin #4" (Tempting Christ)

1 Corinthian 10:6-9

Now these things were our examples, to the intent we should not lust after evil things, as they also lusted. Neither be ye idolaters, as were some of them; as it is written. The people sat down to eat and drink, and rose up to play. Neither let us commit fornication, as some of them committed, and fell in one day three and twenty thousand. Neither let us tempt Christ, as some of them also tempted, and were destroyed of serpents.

Tempting Christ! Can anyone really tempt Christ? As far as I know, according to the dictionary (Merriam Webster) to tempt means 1) to entice to do wrong by promise of pleasure or gain; 2) to provoke. So are we able to entice our Lord and Savior to do wrong or provoke Him? Well, before we answer those questions, let's look at the Biblical definition for "tempting Christ," which is demanding that God do what is contrary to His will! Now that makes sense! Enticing Jesus or provoking Him is automatically contrary to His nature. So when we "tempt Christ" we are demanding that He do something contrary to His will for our selfish benefit. A prime example is asking God to punish the judge who doesn't give us a favorable decision in court or praying that the Lord will break our lawyer's legs because of improper representation. How about this one, asking God to cause our girlfriend or wife to have a car accident if she goes out while we are away! Sound crazy? Well that's exactly how we pray at times, subsequently tempting Christ. Even lying and cheating and then expecting God to bless and prosper us is tempting Christ. Make sure that your study the Scriptures in today's devotion so that your spirit will be encouraged and you won't "tempt Christ."

Additional Reading: Luke 4:9-12; Deuteronomy 6:16; Numbers 21:4-6; Acts 5:1-9

Soul Check

Are you tempting Christ?

Confession

I will not tempt Christ.

Day 50

"Major Sin #5" (Murmuring)

1 Corinthians 10:6-10

Now these things were our examples, to the intent we should not lust after evil things, as they also lusted. Neither be ye idolaters, as were some of them; as it is written. The people sat down to eat and drink, and rose up to play. Neither let us commit fornication, as some of them committed, and fell in one day three and twenty thousand. Neither let us tempt Christ, as some of them also tempted, and were destroyed of serpents. Neither murmur ye, as some of them also murmured, and were destroyed of the destroyer.

As we look at the last of the five major sins that kept the children of Israel out of their Canaan land and also keeps us from having a Canaan land experience in every area of our lives, remember that these were written for our examples. Murmuring is not a term we use today, so most folks don't have a clue to what it means. Murmuring is complaining or whining. The Biblical definition is negative confession. Because we live in a society that has trained us to think the worst and is saturated with all kinds of negativity, it's not wonder that our lives are filled with negative confession. We murmur and complain daily about so many things until I believe that we indulge in this sin more than the others. We murmur on our jobs, in our marriages, to our children and to our friends, concerning our finances. We complain about spiritual leadership, our bosses and even God's Word! Negative confession means that we are cursing (not blessing) the things or people involved. We even murmur against every legal or penal aspect and then want God to bless us in them. Let's watch out for this sin in our lives and bless rather than curse what we speak out of our mouths. Hallelujah!!!

Additional Reading: Deuteronomy 1:27; Numbers 12:1, 10; Numbers 21: 5, 6

Soul Check

Are you murmuring?

Confession

I will not murmur.

Day 51

"Sinning Against God"

Luke 15: 21

And the son said unto him, Father, I have sinned against heaven, and in thy sight, and am no more worthy to be called thy son.

When most of us think about having sinned against someone, we think of having done it against everybody and anybody except God. We tend to seek forgiveness from God, yet we don't repent for having sinned against Him. Usually we feel that we have sinned against a person or persons, but never against the Almighty. Yet, the Scriptures are very clear that when we sin it is "sinning against God," no matter who is involved. When the prodigal son returned home after squandering his money, he said "... Father, I have sinned against heaven and in your sight ... ". And when David began to repent for his sins, though there were several people involved he said in Psalm 51, "Against you, You only have I sinned ..." Everyone should be very mindful when having some quiet or prayer time in their cell or cubicle to not only repent for the people they hurt, but also to seek forgiveness from the Lord for "sinning against" Him. Better yet, when we find ourselves in any compromising position, let us do like Joseph and say, even before we sin, "How can I do this great wickedness and sin against God?" Remember, when we sin against anyone, we are sinning against God.

Additional Reading: Luke 15:11-24; Genesis 39:1-23; Psalm 51

Soul Check

Have you sinned against God?

Confession

Father, forgive me for sinning against you. I repent according to 1 John 1:9.

Day 52

"Seven Abominations"

Proverbs 6:16-19

These six things doth the Lord hate: yes, seven are an abomination unto him: A proud look, a lying tongue, and hands that shed innocent blood. An innocent heart that deviseth wicked imaginations, feet that be swift in running to mischief. A false witness that speaketh lies, and he that soweth discord among the brethren.

Abomination isn't a word that we use frequently in our conversations if we use it at all. It's one of those words that we bypass in our reading, thinking, "We will never have use of it so why look it up." Well, because it's a word that the Lord uses in the Old Testament, I think it's worth looking up and even studying. Anytime a word can be equated with hate, then it should deserve our attention. What is an "abomination?" It's something that is odious, loathsome, detestable and disgusting. In a Biblical sense, it is a deep-seated hatred of something or someone. As Christians, we sometimes tend to place sin in degrees, not fully realizing that sin is sin. We think some outward sins are more serious than some of the inward ones. Yet, the Lord places some of the sins of the spirit (inward) above some of the more obvious ones such as murder. As a matter of fact, at the top of the list is pride and then lying. We are going to look at these seven sins that are an abomination to the Lord and try to ascertain why they are listed the way they are in Proverbs 6:16-19. As we study them for the next seven days, let's pray that we will have the same attitude the Lord has towards them and purpose in our hearts not to take them lightly. Thank you, Jesus!

Soul Check

Is your walk before God an abomination, or is it pleasing in His sight?

Confession

Holy Spirit, expose in me any abominations.

Day 53

"Abomination #1 – Pride"

Proverbs 6:16-19

These six things doth the Lord hate: yes, seven are an abomination unto him: A proud look, a lying tongue, and hands that shed innocent blood. An innocent heart that deviseth wicked imaginations, feet that be swift in running to mischief. A false witness that speaketh lies, and he that soweth discord among the brethren.

Isn't it amazing that the number one abomination from God's perspective is "pride?" Not only does verse 16 speak on "pride" but the Scriptures, especially the Proverbs, are filled with truths relating to pride. More than one devotion will be needed to cover this subject. However, today, we just want to look at why the Lord hates it so much. Well, first of all, pride is the very sin that caused Satan's downfall. Instead of being the worship leader in heaven that the Lord had assigned him, he wanted to be worshipped. He challenged God's sovereignty and became puffed up with himself. I would suggest that we study this section of Scripture (Ezekiel 28:12-19 so that we won't allow this selfish spirit of pride to seduce us. A prideful person is one who is in opposition to God. Pride is conceit, arrogance, disdain and haughty behavior. Pride ruins relationships, destroys fellowship with other believers and builds walls. God resists the proud but gives grace to the humble. There are examples of prideful men who fell just as hard as Satan but who had sense enough to repent. We will discuss some of those examples in the days ahead, but for now remember that pride is an abomination to God, and one of the seven things He hates the most.

Additional Reading: Ezekiel 28:12-19; James 4:6; 1 Peter 5:5

Soul Check

Are you prideful?

Confession

Lord, forgive me for being prideful. Holy Spirit, teach me how to be humble.

Day 54

"Abomination #2 – Lying"

These six things doth the Lord hate: yes, seven are an abomination unto him: A proud bok, a lying tongue, and hands that shed innocent blood. An innocent heart that deviseth wicked imaginations, feet that be swift in running to mischief. A false witness that speaketh lies, and he that soweth discord among the brethren.

Though pride tops the list of things God hates the most, I sense that lying is just a serious. I know for a fact that it is just as devastating, just as deceitful, just as cancerous and just as hurtful as pride is. God hates lying, mainly because telling a lie perverts His Word (truth). It also is the second of the dual sins (pride and lying) which caused the fall of Satan. Satan actually means *slanderer*. We need to pay close attention to this abomination because it is so deceitful and subtle that if we don't stand and walk in truth at all times, it will creep in our psyche and imprison our minds before we know it! It will sear our consciences and become a second nature to us if we aren't careful. Lying, like pride, can be masqueraded and veiled in half-truth even in the lives of the believers. And anyone with any common sense knows that a half-truth is a whole lie. The deceitfulness of lying is that we fool ourselves by saying, "It's okay to tell a little white lie" and get away with it as long as it's not major lying. Hey, there are no degrees of sin, so there are no degrees of lying. None of it is acceptable to God and shouldn't be acceptable to us. Check out the devotion on "Whaling," and others that will deal with this subject. Let's follow Scriptural advice, and stop lying and speak truth with one another. Remember it's truth, not lying, that sets us free. Thank you, Jesus!

Additional Reading: Ephesians 4:25; Zechariah 8:16; John 8:44

Soul Check

Are you a liar?

Confession

Lord, forgive me for being a liar. I purpose in my heart to be truthful.

Day 55

"Abomination #3 – Hands that shed innocent blood."

Proverbs 16:6-9

These six things doth the Lord hate: yes, seven are an abomination unto him: A proud look, a lying tongue, and hands that shed innocent blood. An innocent heart that deviseth wicked imaginations, feet that be swift in running to mischief. A false witness that speaketh lies, and he that soweth discord among the brethren.

Now we come to the outward sins that are more obvious than the inward ones. However, this particular "abomination" is heavily influenced by inward sins such as hatred, bitterness, envy, selfishness and strife. Notice, though, that the sin is described as "hands that shed innocent blood." Now, I don't know what that may mean to you, but to me it is that which is unprovoked and unnecessary. Don't misunderstand me, I believe that God frowns on all types of murder and killing, mainly because it's His will that "all men are saved and come to a knowledge of truth." But when it comes to "hands that shed innocent blood, the Lord becomes furious. I think of abortion as one example of "hands that shed innocent blood." Or what about the ones the Holy Spirit leads us to witness to, and we don't because we feel they are beyond being saved. That is a form of hands that shed innocent blood. I know that there are probably many more examples that fall into this category, but I think we all get the point. So, saints of God, remember that the Lord Jesus Christ came so that we could have life and life more abundantly. Let us put forth every effort to please and glorify Him by refraining from indulging in the Seven Things God Hates the Most."

Additional Reading: Isaiah 1:15; Deuteronomy 5:17; 1 Timothy 2:4; John 10:10

Soul Check

Have your hands participated in the shedding of innocent blood?

Confession

Lord, forgive me for allowing my hands to shed innocent blood. Have mercy on my soul.

Day 56

"Abomination #4 – A Heart that Devises Wicked Plans."

Proverbs 16:16-19

These six things doth the Lord hate: yes, seven are an abomination unto him: A proud look, a lying tongue, and hands that shed innocent blood. An innocent heart that deviseth wicked imaginations, feet that be swift in running to mischief. A false witness that speaketh lies, and he that soweth discord among the brethren.

No matter what your station in life is, no matter what type of environment you grew up in and no matter what your spiritual preferences may have been, we all have this one thing in common; that we all have been guilty of sin. Not only are we born into sin with a heart that thinks evil all the time, but we also live in a world that has trained and conditioned us to think the worst at all times. Plus, we are surrounded by so much negativity, until it's almost like a second nature for us to let our "heart devise wicked plans." Jeremiah tells us that our heart is deceitful above all things and desperately wicked.... So knowing that this sin is an abomination to our Lord, what can we do to make our hearts right before Him? Well, first of all we must acknowledge that we need His help to make it right. Secondly, since we are surely powerless to change on our own, we must yield, surrender and submit our heart to Him. Thirdly, let's "hide His word in our hearts so that we won't sin against Him." Finally, we can follow the wisdom of Proverbs 4:23 and "keep (guard) your heart with all diligence ..." More on the heart in future devotions.

Additional Reading: Jeremiah 17:9-10; Genesis 6:5; Psalm 119:11

Soul Check

What is in your heart?

Prayer

Lord, cleanse my heart so that I can hide Your Word and sin not against You.

Day 57

"Abomination #5 – Feet that are Swift to Running to Evil"

Proverbs 16:16-19

These six things doth the Lord hate: yes, seven are an abomination unto him: A proud look, a lying tongue, and hands that shed innocent blood. An innocent heart that deviseth wicked imaginations, feet that be swift in running to mischief. A false witness that speaketh lies, and he that soweth discord among the brethren.

Some of us, whether in an institutional setting or not, probably have never paid much attention to this abomination. However, most of the prison and jail population are there because of "feet that are swift in running to evil." Just think about how much in a hurry you were to get out of the house and go to hang out with your friends who also had "feet that are swift to running to evil." Now you regret not listening to your wife, your girl or your mother when they tried to get you to stay home the day you got arrested. You ignored their pleas, and now you are suffering the consequences. Had you thought about what you did before you did it, you might have chosen differently. Even after the Lord had helped you out several times when you cried out to Him, you still were in a hurry to do evil. There probably is no limit to the thoughts you must have been thinking, and the majority of your behavior is a result of those negative thoughts. I don't have to elaborate on this topic any more, because everyone knows about "feet that are swift to running to evil." Let's just repent for that sin, meditate upon the Scriptures for today's devotion, and praise God for delivering us from this abomination.

Additional Reading: Isaiah 59:7, 8; Romans 3:15; Proverbs 1:16

Soul Check

Are your feet swift in running to evil?

Prayer

Lord, forgive me for letting my feet be swift in running to evil. Holy Spirit, help me to run towards good.

Day 58

"Abomination # 6 – A False Witness Who Speaks Lies"

Proverbs 6:16-19

These six things doth the Lord hate: yes, seven are an abomination unto him: A proud look, a lying tongue, and hands that shed innocent blood. An innocent heart that deviseth wicked imaginations, feet that be swift in running to mischief. A false witness that speaketh lies, and he that soweth discord among the brethren.

Not only is the sin in today's devotion an abomination to God, but it is also abhorred by many, for nobody likes "a false witness who speaks lies." The main reason our judicial agencies and our law enforcement agencies are so messed up and perverted is due to this abomination. Even in our world of commerce both nationally and internationally, many corporations have been affected by this sin. So much of our history has been distorted, changed and rearranged because of this sin. The Bible gives you several examples of "a false witness who speaks lies" and admonishes us not to participate in such practices. "A false witness who speaks lies" not only is the culprit behind failed relationships, but also is the cause many people are falsely sent to prisons, as well as causing financial ruin for many. So much devastation has resulted because of this sin in the past and today that it's no wonder the Lord calls it an abomination. Let's concentrate on speaking truth at all times and showing love for our brothers and our fellow man. Selah!

Additional Reading: Psalm 27:12; Matthew 26:60-61; Psalm 35:11

Soul Check

Are you a false witness who speaks lies?

Prayer

Lord, forgive me for being a false witness who speaks lies. Holy Spirit, help me to be a true witness and one who speaks the truth.

Day 59

"Abomination #7 – Sowing Discord among the Brothers"

Proverbs 6:16-19

These six things doth the Lord hate: yes, seven are an abomination unto him: A proud look, a lying tongue, and hands that shed innocent blood. An innocent heart that deviseth wicked imaginations, feet that be swift in running to mischief. A false witness that speaketh lies, and he that soweth discord among the brethren.

Now, here is a sin that is so deceptive that it can go unnoticed until it has caused more damage than can be repaired. "Sowing discord among the brothers" is a sin that we take very lightly and rarely discuss or preach it. Yet, God says it's an abomination to Him. Therefore, it would serve us well to take note of this particular sin, since it runs rather rampant in many of our present-day congregations. A seditious spirit is at the root of this sin, and sedition is undermining the constituted authority of a individual. For example, the praise and worship leader goes to the pastor and says, "Pastor, I've been working on this special play that I feel we should do on Resurrection weekend." After much prayer and thought, the pastor informs the praise and worship leader that it's really not a good time. Angrily, the praise and worship leader tells the choir, "We have an excellent play, but we can't do it because the pastor won't let us." That's sedition; yes that's "sowing discord among the brothers." Rather than committing this sin, let us be determined to have a spirit of unity and love among the brothers. We can accomplish so much more for the Kingdom of God when we are in agreement. Thank you, Holy Spirit.

Additional Reading: Acts 15:2; Galatians 5:19-22; Ephesians 4:13

Soul Check

Are you sowing discord among the brothers?

Prayer

Lord, forgive me for sowing discord among the brothers. Holy Spirit, help me to sow unity with my brothers.

Day 60

"U Got the Power"

John 1:12

But as many as received him, to them gave he power to become the sons of God, even to them that believe in his name.

The Bible says in John 1:12 that "As many as received Him, to them He gave the power to become children of God, to those who believe in His name." The terms the Greeks used to describe power in the New Testament are exousia and dunamis. Exousia means authority or the right to do something, whereas dunamis is the literal power. We get our word dynamite from the Greek dunamis. Everyone, whether in prison literally, emotionally, mentally or spiritually, wants the power to overcome. Well, fret no more because our heavenly Father, Jehovah Omnipotent has given all power (exousia and dunamis) to His son Christ Jesus. He in turn takes the same power that's given to Him and gives it to us who believe Him and receive- Him. So no matter who or what imprisons you, you have the power to overcome. Yet, we are more than conquerors, according to Romans 8:39, so we don't just overcome, but we conquer through the creative power that God gave to us when He created us in His image. (More about this in our devotion titled Creative Power). It's very important to remember and appropriate the power Jesus gave us when we are confronted with issues from the penal, legal, and judicial system. Thank God, "U got the power," the Power that is greater than any man, government or system; that has ever existed or will exist on this earth. Hallelujah!!!

Additional Reading: Matthew 28:18; Luke 10:19; Romans 8:37

Soul Check

Do you have the power?

Prayer

Lord, I receive you and believe in your name. Holy Spirit, teach me how to walk in the power that has been given to me as a son of God.

Day 61

"Having A Party"

Luke 15:22-23

But the father said to his servants, Bring forth the best robe, and put it on him; and put a ring on his hand, and shoes on his feet: And bring hither the fatted calf, and kill it; and let us eat, and be merry.

Whenever I reminisce about the music I grew up with, I often start humming some of the tunes from Rock & Roll greats: Balladeers like Jackie Wilson, Otis Redding and my all-time favorite, Sam Cooke. One of Sam's #1 hits was "Having a Party." Not only do I catch myself humming that tune, but also thinking about all the waist-line parties and block parties we used to have back in the Sixties. And growing up in Brooklyn, New York, we knew how to party. But _now that I'm a Christian, I couldn't think of "Having a Party" better than the one they had when the prodigal son returned home from his backslidden condition. Man, they not only welcomed him back with open arms, but the father's love and forgiveness was beyond what anyone had seen or imagined. The father could have been upset and angry with the son. He could have been so disappointed with him that he could have punished him. But instead, he celebrated his return by "Having a Party." It's the same in heaven when one sinner repents. All the angels in heaven rejoice over that one sinner. Yes, my friend, they are "Having a Party!" If you have been like the prodigal son and want to come back home but the devil is whispering in your ear that you aren't welcome, don't listen to him. Because the moment you take one step in the direction of home, preparations for your party have already begun. Praise God!

Additional Reading: Luke 15: 12-3; Luke 15:7; Luke 15:10

Soul Check

Are you ready to come home (back to the Lord)?

Prayer

Lord, forgive me for turning away. I repent of my sins and I am ready to come home! Let the party begin!

Day 62

"Take the Weight Off"

Hebrews 12:1-2

Wherefore seeing we also are compassed about with so great a cloud of witnesses, let us lay aside every weight, and the sin which doth so easily beset us, and let us run with patience the race that is set before us. Looking unto Jesus the author and finisher of our faith; who for the joy that was set before him endured the cross, despising the shame, and is set down at the right hand of the throne of God.

The average person who has been incarcerated for more than two months usually has gained weight during this time. The average weight gained is approximately twenty pounds and the longer the stay, the more weight gained. But this is literal weight that can be controlled through diet and exercise. However, the "weight" spoken of in today's devotion refers to things that weigh us down, some that aren't necessarily sinful. Legal cases can weigh you down; financial woes, separation from family and love ones also can weigh you down. Then there's the pressure from the controlled environment itself, as well as the mental anguish you experience. All of this takes its toll on you, but the good news is that you can "take the weight off!" How does one accomplish this spiritual feat? With proper diet and exercise. The proper diet is to feed on the Word of God daily and the proper exercise is to meditate upon that which God is revealing to you. You can "take the weight off" and keep it off with the help of the Holy Spirit. Remember saints that the Lord never asks us to do something we can't do. So when He says, "Take the weight off," just do it and watch how good you will feel. Hallelujah!!!

Additional Reading: Matthew 11:29; Matthew 4:4; Joshua 1:8

Soul Check

What "weight" do you need to let go of?

Prayer

Holy Spirit, grant me the courage and strength to be able to lay aside the "weights" that so easily beset me.

Day 63

"The Choice is Yours"

Joshua 24:15

And if it seem evil unto you to serve the Lord, choose you this day whom ye will serve; whether the gods which your fathers served that were on the other side of the flood, or the gods of the Amorites, in whose land ye dwell: but as for me and my house, we will serve the Lord.

Unlike some traditional religions that force one to serve certain gods, Christianity always gives you a choice. This premise is in keeping with the principle that God set forth in Deut 30:19. Unlike any other part of his creation, we are the only one created in His image and given the power of choice. I firmly believe that the choices we make in life are predicated upon the God we serve. Joshua tells the children of Israel just before they settle down in the Promised Land that "the choice is yours." "You can serve the gods your forefathers serve on the other side of the river or the gods of the Amorites in whose land you dwell ..." God never forces Himself on anyone and doesn't want His servants forcing Him on anyone. "The choice is yours." You can't serve God because your parents serve Him. You can't worship and serve God because your friends do or because it's the latest fad. No, you have to make a choice to serve Him. Despite all that you have been through, no matter what your present situation is or isn't, "the choice is yours." Join me in the spirit of Joshua who told them, "As for me and my house, we will serve the Lord!"

Additional Reading: Deuteronomy 30:19

Soul Check

Who will you serve? The choice is yours.

Prayer

Lord, I choose to serve You.

Day 64

"Are You Hungry?"

Matthew 5:6

Blessed are they which do hunger and thirst after righteousness for they shall be filled.

Whenever I think about a natural hunger, I automatically think of some of my favorite restaurants. Then I start to dwell on some of my favorite dishes. And if my money isn't right, I then think about some of my favorite cooks in my family. Then when it's all said and done, it usually boils down to what my favorite cook (my wife) is preparing for us. The power of suggestion makes you hungry even when you haven't been thinking about food. Oh, how I wish that same power of suggestion would make me hungry for spiritual food as it does for natural food. Because when you develop an appetite for spiritual food you can open the Word of God and receive a smorgasbord of heavenly manna that will fill you up. Are you hungry, not just for the things of God, but the deep things of God? If so, then I suggest you set your table with the Word of God, some devotional material and maybe some other spiritual resource material that you know lines up with the Word and will of God, and have yourself a feast. Whatever you do, don't lose your hunger and thirst for righteousness. "Are you hungry?" Selah

Additional Reading: Matthew 4:4; Daniel 1:8; Job 23:12

Soul Check

What do you hunger for?

Prayer

Lord, increase my desire to hunger and thirst for your righteousness.

Day 65

"A Prison of Denial"

Genesis 3:9-12

And the Lord God called unto Adam and said unto him, Where art thou? And he said, I heard thy voice in the garden, and I was afraid, because I was naked; and I hid myself. And he said, Who told thee that thou wast naked? Has thou eaten of the tree, whereof I commanded thee that thou shouldest not eat? And the man said, The woman whom thou gavest to be with me, she gave me of the tree, and I did eat.

I think that many times in our Christian journey, we must go all the way back to Adam in order to truly understand how his sin continues to affect us today. Take, for instance, the sin of denial. Many of us may not even consider it a sin, but believe me, it is the cousin of lying. In the Garden of Eden when God first approached Adam about his disobedience, instead of accepting responsibility, he denied it saying, "The woman you gave me gave it to me and I ate." Genesis 3:9-12. Instead of just accepting responsibility for his actions, he began a process and practice of placing us in "a prison of denial." Attached to this process is placing the blame on others. All throughout the history of mankind, man has repeatedly felt trapped in "a prison of denial. It is so deeply ingrained in us that it's going to take the help of the Holy Spirit to get us freedom from this prison of denial. Denial causes many offenders to play the blame game and not deal with the issues that are hindering their growth. It also continually feeds their pride. Look how Peter denied the Lord and ended up in a prison of denial until the Lord set him free and restored him. Thank God, there's a way out of this prison of denial.

Additional Reading: John 18:17, 25, 27; 2 Timothy 3:5; 2 Timothy 2:16

Soul Check

Are you in a prison of denial?

Prayer

Lord, I accept responsibility for my actions. Please set me free from my prison of denial.

Day 66

"In His Right Mind"

Mark 5:15

And they come to Jesus, and see him that was possessed with the devil, and had the legion, sitting, and clothed, and in his right mind: and they were afraid.

Have you ever wondered why there is so much mental illness today? Well, I believe that it has a lot to do with demonic oppression or possession. As the woman of God, Joyce Meyer, says, "The battlefield is in the mind." As in the account of the man who lived in the tombs, over 2,000 demonic spirits possessed him, so much until they had to take on a group name, Legion! It's funny how the state and federal penal systems gives a psychological and psychiatric profile on every inmate, but never a spiritual one. So when they try to treat the mental illness with medication or psychoanalysis, they have no success. In order to help someone get "in his right mind," you must do as Jesus did and cast the demons out. However, if you are still a babe in Christ, get some spiritual advice from someone in leadership in the church before you try to cast out demons from yourself or anyone else. It's nothing to play with, but the rewards for someone set free, clothed and "in his right mind" are out of this world (heavenly). I personally know what it's like to be oppressed by the devil, so bad until you think you are possessed. But, thank God, that through the blood of Jesus, I got delivered, and now through His grace and love, I am clothed and "in my right mind."

Additional Reading: Mark 5:1-19; Daniel 4:34; 2 Timothy 1:7; Luke 8:35

Soul Check

Are you in your right mind?

Prayer

Lord deliver me from any oppressive or possessive spirits. I want to be clothed in my right mind.

Day 67

"Void of Manners"

1 Thessalonians 5:18

In everything give thanks: for this is the will of God in Christ Jesus concerning you.

Never before in all of my fifty-five years have I seen such a "void of manners" like I see today. And, contrary to popular opinion, it isn't just the younger generation. Where we lost it concerning our manners and just having a sense of common courtesy, I don't know. What I do know is that the majority of people, especially the younger generation, acts as though you owe them something. Yes, it's even prevalent in the church at large. Nobody says "thank you", "yes, sir, no, sir", "please", or "excuse me" anymore; they have to be reminded when they do say them. Maybe I'm just a little old fashioned, but it was mandatory for us to display manners when I was growing up. My generation wasn't "void of manners;" as a matter of fact, we probably had too many. Why there is such an ungrateful and unthankful attitude in today's society, I don't know. I do know that according to Scripture, the Lord wants us to be thankful in all situations. I'm also reminded of the ten lepers that were healed and how only one came back to thank Jesus for his healing. I believe that he maintained his healing due to the fact that he was grateful. Let's see what the Lord would have us to do to maintain an attitude of gratitude, and encourage others to do the same. God bless!

Additional Reading: Luke 17:11-19; 2 Timothy 3:1-5; Romans 1:21

Soul Check

Are you void of manners?

Prayer

Holy Spirit, convict me when I am not grateful and when I do not display any manners.

Day 68

"Great Benefits"

Psalm 103:2-5

Bless the Lord, O my soul, and forget not all his benefits: Who forgiveth all thine iniquities; who healeth all thy diseases; who redeemeth life from destruction; who crowneth thee with lovingkindness and tender mercies; who satisfieth thy mouth with good things; so that thy youth is renewed like the eagle's.

One of the first things that we look for when inquiring about an employment or career is the benefits they offer! Some businesses, corporations and even the church offer some amazing benefits, while other's don't offer any at all, including health and dental insurance. The main reason we look for these "great benefits" is because they provide us with a certain amount of insurance. The only negative is that there is never a guarantee that you will receive the promised benefits. Sometimes the co-pay is so high that it's not a benefit at all. With all of the uncertainties surrounding the benefits the world has to offer, some of the "great benefits" aren't so great after all. However, when it comes to the benefits the Lord has to offer, especially the insurance He provides, now you are really talking "great benefits." Just look at the list in Psalm 103:2-9. And the insurance is eternal, because the benefits the Lord has to offer never fail or go bankrupt. Plus, the Bible says "that He daily loads us with benefits," so whatever we need, we have. Yes, the guarantee from the benefits God has for us truly makes them "great benefits." Glory to God!

Additional Reading: Psalm 103:2-9; Psalm 116:12; Psalm 68:19; 2 Peter 1:3-4

Soul Check

Have you forgotten the benefits of the Lord?

Prayer

Lord, thank you for the "great benefits"!

Day 69

"K.I.S.S."

2 Corinthians 1:12; 11:3

For our rejoicing is this, the testimony of our conscience, that in simplicity and godly sincerity, not with fleshly wisdom, but by the grace of God, we have had our conversation in the world, and more abundantly to you-ward. But I fear, lest by any means, as the serpent beguiled Eve through his subtly, so your minds should be corrupted from the simplicity that is in Christ.

Many of us at first glance would immediately think this acronym stood for "keep it simple, stupid," since that's what it is popularly known for. However, we can't always take for granted certain acronyms, since some of them have different meanings. For instance, "A.A." can stand for Alcoholics Anonymous or Associate in Arts. Sometimes we purposely change them for our own need. Such is today's devotion. The "K.I.S.S." acronym stands for "keep it simple, saints." I changed the last word for two reasons: Number one, I didn't want to insult anyone by referring to them as stupid. Secondly, it targets my audience for today's devotion. So many times we, through our own rationalization, our pseudo-intellect and our misguided knowledge tend to complicate the gospel. People tend to walk away confused when we make it sound so complex. Jesus always kept it simple. When He spoke to farmers, He talked about seeds, sowing and reaping. When He talked to fisherman, He used terms like nets, boats, and fish. He wanted them to understand what He was saying to them, so no matter how prophetic, profound or prolific it was, He always "K.I.S.S.". So remember today's Scriptural verse, and let's do our best to follow in His footsteps and "K.I.S.S." Selah!

Additional Reading: Romans 12:8; 1 Corinthians 2:4-5

Soul Check

Are you "K.I.S.S."?

Prayer

Holy Spirit, teach me how to "K.I.S.S."!

Day 70

"Abandonment"

2 Timothy 4:16-17

At my first answer no man stood with me, but all men forsook me: I pray God that it may not be laid to their charge. Notwithstanding the Lord stood with me, and strengthened me; that by me the preaching might be fully known, and that all the Gentiles might hear: and I was delivered out of the mouth of the lion.

To those who have been incarcerated for a long time – do you feel abandoned? Do you find yourself getting upset when you think of those who have given up on you completely? Do you even as a Christian feel that you have a right to be angry at the ones who deserted you? Or do you seek revenge upon those who have forsaken you? Well, have I got news for you! All of these emotions you may be having about "abandonment" might seem quite legit. Mainly, to be "forsaken", "deserted", and "given up on completely" isn't pleasant, to say the least. I imagine how difficult it must have been for Jesus when He cried out, "Father, Father why hast thou forsaken me? (Matthew 27:46) And what about the apostle Paul when he felt deserted by everyone except the Lord? (2 Timothy 4:16-17) Man of God, Woman of God, you may rightfully have these feelings of abandonment, but I encourage you to let it go. Think about those who feel abandoned by you because of your incarceration: wives, children and other family members and friends. Yes, this whole issue of abandonment is ugly, but the good news is that we can shake it off, because the Lord has promised that He would "never leave us nor forsake us." That alone should be enough to deliver you from any feelings or thoughts of abandonment. Praise the Lord.

Additional Reading: Hebrews 13:5; Psalm 37:25; John 16:32

Soul Check

Do you have feelings or thoughts of abandonment? Shake it off; let it go!

Prayer

Lord, heal me of abandonment. I forgive those who have abandoned me, and forgive me for those that I have abandoned.

Day 71

"Lean on Him"

Psalm 91:15

He shall call upon me, and I will answer him: I will be with him in trouble; I will deliver him, and honour him.

Bill Withers in his very popular song, "Lean on Me," had a particular verse that captured just about everyone's attention. You could tell, because many were caught humming or singing this one verse or stanza. "Lean on me, when you're not strong, and I'll be your friend, I'll help you carry on, for it won't be long, til I'm gonna need somebody to lean on!" Most of the rest of the song was either hummed along, or incorrect words were inserted because the original ones were forgotten. But not the above quoted verse --everyone had that down pat, and it was sung more than what was in the song itself. I imagine everyone felt good about having someone to lean on in a time of crisis. So I don't knock the song, because it's truly one of my favorites. I just want you to know that there is someone you can lean on at all times, someone who says "... Lo, I am with you always, even to the end of time." Yes, when you "lean on Him" you will sense a security, protection and peace that you have never felt or sensed before. No, He's not any contemporary character in a song or movie. He is the real deal, our Lord and Savior, Jesus Christ. When you lean on Him, you gain the strength you need to be strong and courage so that someone can now lean on you.

Additional Reading: Psalm 91; Matthew 28:20; Acts 18:10; Jeremiah 1:8

Soul Check

Who are you leaning on?

Prayer

Holy Spirit, teach me how to lean on Him!

Day 72

"Failing Isn't the Worst Thing"

Joshua 1:5

There shall not any man be able to stand before thee all the days of thy life: as I was with Moses, so I will be with thee: I will not fail thee, nor forsake thee.

Most of us fail many times, and as for that person who claims they never fail—well, then they must be Jesus. For He alone is the only one I know of whom the Bible says, He never failed. What matters the most and something we need to come to grips with is that "failing isn't the worst thing, quitting is." God knows we are going to fail, but as long as we don't quit, then He always has something to work with. It's when we quit that we actually have taken Him out of the equation so that He has nothing to work with on our behalf. Society condemns us and labels us as failures whenever we get into trouble or make a mistake. But others' thoughts and feelings about us don't dictate who we really are or the potential we still have to be successful. And no matter how many times you may have failed, there still dwells in you the ability and the potential to succeed. God spoke words of encouragement to us as well as to men of old, letting us know that we could make it. Paul didn't think that "failing was the worst thing," That's why he said, "I can do all things through Christ who strengthens me." So whenever you feel discouraged and the devil tries to condemn you, remember, "Failing isn't the worst thing." Hallelujah to God!

Additional Reading: Joshua 1:5-8; Deuteronomy 31:6-8; Philippians 4:13; 1 Corinthians 13:8

Soul Check

Do you see yourself as a failure?

Prayer

Lord, thank you for your promise that you will never leave me or forsake me and that I can do all things through Christ who strengthens me. I will not quit.

Day 73

"Morally Bankrupt"

Genesis 6:5

And God saw that the wickedness of man was great in the earth, and that every imagination of the thoughts of his heart was only evil continually.

Because the society in which we live_ has taught us to think the worst as well as conditioned us to think negative, we have allowed ourselves to become "morally bankrupt." In one of our devotions, we discussed how our nation has become "void of manners," which I believe is a direct correlation to being "morally bankrupt." It's not just those from the "hood" or those who are impoverished that are filling up our jails and prisons. Also those white collar crimes are at an all time high due to our being morally bankrupt. When I was growing up in New York, you never heard of any mothers harming or killing their children. Neither were so many women gracing our prison halls. And I dare to say that it's not just crime that makes us "morally bankrupt." It's the same-sex marriages, the living together without the benefits of marriage, and legalized abortion, as well as rampant growth of homosexuality. It's the total disregard for human life and the covert racism that is tearing our country apart, declaring us a society that's "morally bankrupt." We have seen it before in the history of man and how the Lord dealt with it. If we ever needed to pray 2 Chronicles 7:14, now is the time, so that we can reverse the curse of being "morally bankrupt" and begin to live the abundant life Jesus gave us.

Additional Reading: Genesis 18:20-21; 1 Corinthians 6:9-11; Psalm 37:20

Soul Check

Are you morally bankrupt?

Prayer

Lord, your Word says that if I humble myself, pray, seek your Face and turn from my wicked ways; then you will hear from heaven, and you will forgive my sin and heal my land.

Day 74

"Mind Stayed On Jesus"

Isaiah 26:3

Thou will keep him in perfect peace, whose mind is stayed on thee: because he trusteth in thee.

I believe that one of the most important steps to our spiritual growth and Christian living is to keep our "mind stayed on Jesus." Before I share with you some of the benefits a quiet mind will produce, let me share with you its importance. In our fast-paced society with all of its modern technology (even in our prisons), there is so much distraction that you really have to discipline your mind. By this, I mean you have to focus your thinking on the positive and not allow your mind to wander so much. If the enemy can distract you, he can defeat you. I know that people don't want to hear the truth anymore, but some of the stuff that they listen to on radio, television, computers, ipods, x-boxes, videos, DVD's, etc. is distracting them from having their "mind stayed on Jesus." Keeping your "mind stayed on Jesus" will help you overcome being distracted as you renew your mind. You can have perfect peace when your mind is stayed on Jesus. I know that most of us think it's difficult to keep our minds constantly focused on Jesus. Well, it's not, because the Word of God says that we have the mind of Christ. That alone should give us the incentive to discipline ourselves so that we can keep our "mind stayed on Jesus." Glory to God!

Additional Reading: Romans 8:6; 1 Corinthians 2:16; 2 Timothy 1:7; Proverbs 16:7; Romans 12:1, 2

Soul Check

Is your mind stayed on Jesus?

Prayer

Lord I purpose in my heart to keep my mind stayed on You!

Day 75

"Follow the Instructions"

Proverbs 4:1

Hear, ye children, the instruction of a father, and attend to know understanding.

Living in such a fast-paced society where everyone wants everything instantly has dubbed us the "microwave generation". Technology, with all of its megabytes and gigabytes, has made our computers and regular households appliances capable of performing at ridiculous speeds until you have to read hundreds of instruction booklets just to keep pace. But because we're in such a hurry, we don't take time to "follow the instructions." That's the way it is with our high-tech gadgets, our cars and even our very lives. Failure to "follow the instructions" can ruin our gadgets and cars, and when it comes to our lives, it can kill us. That's why the Lord is so adamant about adhering to His instructions and getting the right information--because God never gives information (which is optional), but only instructions (which aren't optional). Even in controlled and structured environments, we are told first and foremost to "follow the instructions," and everything will go well. Yet, because we want it our way, when we want it and how we want it, we negate the importance of instructions. My prayer is that no matter what station of life you're in, you will learn the benefits of life when you follow the instructions. Praise God!

Additional Reading: Proverbs 8:33; Proverbs 13:1; 2 Timothy 3:16; Acts 18:25;

Soul Check

Do you follow instructions?

Prayer

Lord, forgive me for wanting my own way. I purpose to follow instructions.

Day 76

"Friends"

John 15:13-15

Greater love hath no man than this, that a man lay down his life for his friends. Ye are my friends, if ye do whatsoever I command you. Henceforth I call you not servants; for the servant knoweth not what his lord doeth: but I have called you friends; for all things that I have heard of my Father I have made known unto you.

Today's devotion is not about the television program by the same name. No, I'm referring to and using two of my best "friends" to illustrate the friendship that the Lord wants to have with us. I have always proposed that people can really determine their relationship with God based on the relationship they have with their brothers in Christ (male & female). So taking this principle and premise a step farther, we can say that "we can determine our friendship with God based on our friendship with one another." I pray that I am right, because I have two of the closest, dearest, truest and loving "friends" in Ron and Donna Fuhrmann. They have not only exemplified the love of God towards me and my family but have also been the "friend that sticks closer than a brother" spoken of in Proverbs 18:24. Without going into depth, I can honestly confess that along with my wife (my best friend), they have shown me what the love of Christ is all about. They have done this through their words and deeds. Pen and paper do an injustice to who they really are. When I think of a definition of friends, Ron and Donna come to mind. We all need friends, so prove yourself friendly and watch the friends the Lord Jesus will bring into your life. What a "friend" we have in Jesus!

Additional Reading: 1 John 4:20-21; Proverb 18:24; Proverb 17:17; James 2:23; 2 Chronicles 20:7

Soul Check

Do you have a "friend(s)" that sticks closer than a brother?

Prayer

Lord, show me how to be friendly so that I may have friends!

Day 77

"U-R-Full"

Matthew 19:28-29

And Jesus said unto them, Verily I say unto you that ye which have followed me, in the regeneration when the Son of man shall sit in the throne of his glory, ye also shall sit upon twelve thrones, judging the twelve tribes of Israel. And every one that hath forsaken houses, or brethren, or sisters, or father, or mother, or wife, or children, or lands for my name's sake, shall receive an hundredfold, and shall inherit everlasting life.

It is funny how sometimes unsaved folks will say something that is truly Biblical and not even know it. The topic for today's devotion is a classic example. Much of the slang in the streets as well as in the prisons include the phrase "U-R-Full" or he and she are full, meaning that they are supposedly doing well financially and materially. You may be wondering what this has got to do with anything spiritual. Well, read on, because I was amazed when I saw the term in the Bible for the first time. Turn with me to 1 Corinthians 4:8. What does it mean--U-R-Full"--in the spiritual sense? Well, if in the natural it means you are well off financially and materially, then it has even greater affect in the spiritual. What the world has in the natural is subject to rust and decay, whereas what we have is eternal. What do we have that makes us so full? Well, if we "seek first His Kingdom and His righteousness (spiritual), then we will have all these things (natural) added to us." So we have everything we need, both in this world and in the next. Look at what Jesus said about that as you review the Scriptures for today's devotion. Then you will realize that if indeed you have Jesus Christ as your Lord and Saviour, then "U-R-Full," not just with natural, tangible things but more importantly "full" of His Spirit. Praise God!

Additional Reading: Mark 10:29-31; Matthew 6:32-33; Psalm 37:25; Ephesians 5:18

Soul Check

Are you full?

Prayer

Lord, I will seek first the Kingdom of God and all Your righteousness.

Day 78

"It's Not My Fault"

2 Corinthian 12:9-10

And he said unto me, My grace is sufficient for thee: for my strength is made perfect in weakness. Most gladly therefore will I rather glory in my infirmities, that the power of Christ may rest upon me. Therefore I take pleasure in infirmities, in reproaches, in necessities, in persecutions, in distresses for Christ's sake: for when I am weak, then am I strong.

How many times have we said this growing up? I know that I probably have worn the statement out both as a child and as an adult. I'm not ashamed to admit that I tried escaping my responsibility for whatever went wrong in my life by saying, "It's not my fault." I dare not ask how many have said this and are still claiming it. No, I understand that, because we all have faults and don't like them, then we won't admit them. But_ if we will be truthful with ourselves, we will admit that many times it was our fault. A fault can be characterized as a weakness, failing, an imperfection, impairment or defect - a mistake, a wrong or an error. Let's just use the term "weakness;" then we can see that none of us are immune, and sometimes can be at fault. Yet, whenever I tend to look at my human frailty, I just thank God that "(His) grace is sufficient for me, for (His) strength is made perfect in weakness." Having faults is not the worst thing, but always complaining that "it's not my fault" will keep us imprisoned to a lie. My word of encouragement to us is to trust the Lord to deliver us, repent where it has been our fault and submit totally to the One who can make us strong when we are weak. Focus on the positive things in your life, and watch "it's not my fault" disappear from our mouths, our thoughts and our hearts. Glory Hallelujah!

Additional Reading: 1 Peter 4:12-16; Mark 14:38; Romans 7:18, 21-24

Soul Check

Begin accepting responsibility.

Prayer

Lord, forgive me for not accepting responsibilities for my faults. Your grace is sufficient for me.

Day 79

"Called To Obey"

Matthew 21:28-31

But what think ye? A certain man had two sons; and he came to the first, and said, Son, go work to day in my vineyard. He answered and said, I will not: but afterward he repented, and went. And he came to the second, and said likewise. And he answered and said, I go, sir: and went not.

Now, obedience is a topic that could require many books to be written about it. But I will only highlight a few of its principles. When it comes to Scriptures on obedience, I like the story of the two sons in the gospel of Matthew. There, one son says he will go but doesn't, and the other says he won't go but does. Who did the will of the Father? Of course, it was the one who went. So obedience isn't just what you say but what you do. We are "called to obey," yet it is a difficult calling, because it requires that we submit. And God doesn't just ask us to obey Him and His Word, but also to obey those in authority. Now, the latter is extremely hard for those new converts who are institutionalized. They have always rebelled against authority, so they struggle when it comes to obeying those who have charge_ over them. I like to tell them that since they are now "new creations," they must learn obedience just as Jesus did. And since revelation from God is based on obedience, than they need to submit. If they can't do it in their own strength (which most of us can't), then pray for God's wisdom and power. He's not respecter of persons and will give you what you need to succeed. Just remember, you are called to obey and that calling isn't optional. Thank you, Jesus!

Additional Reading: John 14:15, 21, 23-24; Romans 13:1-2, 2 Corinthians 5:17; Mark 10:27

Soul Check

Are you rebelling against those in authority?

Prayer

Lord, I repent. Holy Spirit, teach me how to obey.

Day 80

"He's Working On You"

Philippians 1:6

Being confident of this very thing, that he which hath begun a good work in you will perform it until the day of Jesus Christ.

Man, when I'm going through situations, and things look as though they are getting worse, the first thing the enemy throws up in my face is, "God's not working in you anymore." As much as I hate to admit it, it seems like he has a valid point. Yet, knowing his nature (liar) and his MO (mode of operation) which is deception, I'm convinced that though I don't see it or sense it, God is still working. I know this beyond a shadow of a doubt, or as Paul would say, "I'm persuaded ..." because he is the one who began the good work in us, not our family, or our friends, not the pastor or the lawyer. They may have influenced the work, but He started it. Not even our wives, parents, children or any social agency are responsible. The "He" in Philippians 1:6 is the great "I Am," the Alpha & Omega, the King of Kings and the Lord of Lords. Yes, "He," not the system or the government, is still working in us. He is the Good Shepherd, the Mighty One, Our Prince of Peace, Our Lord and Savior, Our Kinsman Redeemer, Jehovah Jireh, Jehovah Shalom, Jehovah Nissi, El Elon, the Bright Morning Star, the Rose of Sharon, Wonderful Counselor and our Eternal Father. He started this good work in us and He will carry it on to completion to the day of Jesus Christ. So when it doesn't seem like He's working on your behalf, take your eyes off your situation, and place them on the one who started the good work in you! Amen.

Additional Reading: Philippians 2:13; John 6:29; Hebrews 13:20-21; 2 Thessalonians 1:11

Soul Check

Do you feel like God is not working in your situation?

Prayer

Lord, I confess that You started a good work in me, and You will carry it on to completion.

Day 81

"Inferiority Complex"

Exodus 3:14 and Exodus 4:10-12

And God said unto Moses, I AM THAT I AM: and he said, Thus shalt thou say unto the children of Israel, I AM hath sent me unto you. And Moses said unto the Lord, O My Lord, I am not eloquent, neither heretofore, nor since thou hast spoken unto thy servant: but I am slow of speech, and of a slow tongue. And the Lord said unto him, Who hath made man's mouth? or who maketh the dumb, or deaf, or the seeing, or the blind? have not I the Lord? Now therefore go, and I will be with thy mouth, and teach thee what thou shalt say.

As I have watched and studied some of the behaviors that are displayed in some correctional facilities, I couldn't help but notice how inferior many of the inmates feel, not just physically, mentally, psychologically, and intellectually, but also relationally and spiritually. The more I share with them, the more open and honest they become about their "inferiority complex." I know for a fact that some of it is due to a generational curse, especially in regard to our past history of slavery. Then a good percentage is due to the environment they were brought up in-- neighborhood, housing, schooling, etc. And finally, I believe that the judicial and the penal systems have played a role in helping them develop this complex. It's funny how each individual profession or institution addresses the issue differently, all with good intentions, I'm sure. Yet I can show you a more excellent way, I tell them. Then the more the prisoners with inferiority complexes study the Word of God and pray, the more open they are to the Holy Spirit's leading. Now they are beginning to see themselves as God sees them. They are taking authority over the spirit behind it and renouncing this "inferiority complex" altogether. They know that they are special enough to be engraved in the palm of the Master's hand. They rejoice that they are fearfully and wonderfully made. The revelation of who they are in Christ has prompted them to exchange their "inferiority complex" for the workmanship of Christ!

Additional Reading: Isaiah 49:16; Psalm 139:14; Ephesians 2:10

Soul Check

Are you feeling inferior?

Prayer

Lord, I confess that I am the workmanship of Christ. I no longer feel inferior because Your Word says that I am fearfully and wonderfully made!

Day 82

"Gossiping"

1 Timothy 5:13 Amplified

Moreover, as they go about from house to house, they learn to be idlers, and not only idlers, but gossips and busybodies, saying what they should not say and talking of things they should not mention.

Oh, how I sought to avoid this subject. But in order to do that, one would have to remove themselves from the world. Seriously, though, I don't mind sharing about it as the Spirit of the Lord would move me. I'm just amazed at how much gossiping is done by men, behind prison walls, no less. I mean, it's not as if their social life is unlimited. Plus, I have always felt that "gossiping" was for women and those who drank too much. But I have seen it expand to every sphere and facet of life. So many are engaged in it as a pastime that it could be considered as verbal calisthenics and part of their daily workout routine. I'm not being critical or anything, but the truth of the matter is that "gossiping" is based on the same negative confession as "murmuring." There is nothing but a negative connotation associated with "gossiping." Plus, why would anyone want to habitually reveal personal or sensational facts about someone? Well, I don't know of anyone who is totally immune from this sin. Yes, it is sin, so let us repent and forsake this sort of lifestyle. Let's heed the Biblical warnings and purpose in our hearts to only speak that which is edifying and uplifting about others. What helped me stop was the constant mental reminder that when I talk about someone, I'm talking about God's children and those created in His image. Forgive us, heavenly Father, for any "gossiping" we have done, and cleanse our hearts and our mouths. Thank you, Jesus!

Additional Reading: Leviticus 19:16; Proverbs 11:13; Proverbs 20:19, 1 Peter 4:15

Soul Check

Are you a gossiper?

Prayer

Lord, I repent of this sin. Cleanse my heart and my mouth.

Day 83

"Access Denied"

Hebrew 4:16

Let us therefore come boldly unto the throne of grace, that we may obtain mercy, and find grace to help in time of need.

You know, I'm not as computer literate as I would like to be, but I'm working on it. It seems like the less you know about the software or hardware, the more frustrated you can become, especially when you try to log on, and the system keeps saying, "invalid password," which literally means, "access denied." I think that not being able to get into your own system is the worst that could possibly go wrong. I know for me it is, because once I have made up my mind to do something on the computer, I'm ready to go. So not having "access" to our heavenly Father is not that difficult. As a matter of fact, the Word of God tells us "to come boldly to His throne of grace to find mercy and help in the time of need." So we will never have to worry about being told, "access denied." Thank God, He has an open-door policy that gives us access to Him at all times. Nobody in their right mind wants to hear "access denied," especially when you really need to get to Him. Praise God that His way of doing things is totally different than man's way. Certainly, when you are praying, you want to make sure you have access so that you know your prayers are heard. Accessibility is a good thing; "access denied" is not.

Additional Reading: Ephesians 2:18; Hebrew 10:19-21; 1 John 5:14-15

Soul Check

Do you come boldly to the throne of Grace?

Prayer

Lord, I come boldly to the throne of grace that I may obtain mercy and find grace to help in time of need.

Day 84

"Learned Obedience"

Hebrew 5:8

Though he were a Son, yet learned he obedience by the things which he suffered.

One of our devotions, "Called to Obey," showed us the importance of being obedient to God and to those in authority. After considerable prayer and thought provoking reflections, I began to wonder, "Is it possible for us to walk in obedience at all times?" Considering all of the variables that affect our lives daily, the question remains, can obedience be adhered to completely? Well, we all know that if the Lord says we can do something, that with His help we can. Not only can we "learn obedience," but we can walk in it consistently, just like Jesus did when He walked the earth. I sometimes wonder why the Son of God had to learn anything, since He knows everything. Well, the answer is found in the fact that when "He found Himself in the likeness of man" that He then had to "learn obedience." He being our primary role model let us start to discipline ourselves as we "learn obedience." There's no doubt in my mind that it is possible. The revelation that God gives us in His Word shows us that it is possible, and not only that, but it is do-able (to borrow a phrase from Sean Connery). Since revelation is based on obedience and our spiritual success is predicated on obedience, let us learn obedience and glorify God through it.

Additional Reading: Philippians 2:5-8; Philippians 4:13

Soul Check

Are you being obedient?

Prayer

Lord, I purpose in my heart to be obedient so that You may be glorified.

Day 85

"My Baby's Mama"

Proverbs 22:1

A good name is rather to be chosen than great riches, and loving favour rather than silver and gold.

Having had several conversations where the term "My Baby's Mama" came up, I finally got up enough nerve to inquire about the term. Doesn't your "baby's mama" have a name that will identify her from someone else? Many of the men in the prison system, as well as those on parole or probation, sometimes have more than one child out of wedlock, so it can be confusing as to which girl they are referring to when they say "my baby's mama". It's funny how lightly we take the importance of a name. Names use to have meanings that were important to the parents. Nowadays, the names that are given to babies are what sound cute and nice whether they have meaning or not. However, from God's perspective, names mean a lot and were often given according to relationship with Him. For instance, Abram was changed to Abraham meaning the "father of many." Sarai was changed to Sarah because she was going to be a mother of nations. Jesus' name definitely had meaning: "salvation is with us." So I'm sure that the Lord wants us to be called by our names and not by some street slang that can refer to anyone. The Bible says that "a good name is to be chosen rather than great riches." Even God calls each star by name, so isn't your "baby's mama" deserving of much more? Call her by her name, Hallelujah!

Additional Reading: Ecclesiastes 7:1; Proverb 22:1; Isaiah 40:26; Psalm 147:4

Soul Check

What's your "baby's mama" name?

Prayer

Holy Spirit, convict me every time I say, "My baby's mama!"

Day 86

"Be Yourself"

2 Corinthians 5:17-21

Therefore if any man be in Christ, he is a new creature: old things are passed away; behold, all things are become new. And all things are of God, who hath reconciled us to himself by Jesus Christ, and hath given to us the ministry of reconciliation; To wit, that God was in Christ, reconciling the world unto himself, not imputing their trespasses unto them; and hath committed unto us the word of reconciliation. Now then we are ambassadors for Christ, as though God did beseech you by us: we pray you in Christ's stead, be ye reconciled to God. For he hath made him to be sin for us, who knew no sin, that we might be made the righteousness of God in Him.

Other than serving God and your fellow man, there is nothing you can do greater for the Kingdom than "be yourself." So much time and energy is wasted when one strives to be someone else. God didn't create us to be or imitate anyone else. Some people spend their whole lives trying to be someone else because they have no idea of who they really are. The Lord wants you to "be yourself." Out of the 6 billion people on the planet today, no one can be you better than you can. God has given you gifts, talents, abilities and skills that he didn't give to anyone else. Yes, others heal and maybe prophesy but when it comes to having gifts combined with your personality, there's no comparison. You have uniqueness and a calling on your life like nobody else. So "be yourself!" There are some people that will cross your path that you and only you can witness to. There are generations that will be impacted because of what God has deposited in you and no one else. So many wish they could be you and even strive to be like you, but it's just not possible. Even the greatest look-a-like is only a cheap imitation of a great original, so be yourself. Selah!

Additional Reading: Ephesians 1:5; John 1:12; Ephesians 5:1

Soul Check

Are you being yourself?

Prayer

Lord, I accept who I am because it is You that has formed me.

Day 87

"Repent For Real"

Mark 1:4, 15

John did baptize in the wilderness, and preach the baptism of repentance for the remission of sins. And saying, the time is fulfilled, and the kingdom of God is at hand: repent ye, and believe the gospel.

Considering that the first words Jesus spoke at the beginning of His ministry were "Repent, for the Kingdom of heaven has drawn near," I believe that we all need to get serious about repentance in our lives. Yes, as Christians we need to not just give lip service to repentance but rather "repent for real." True repentance is a turning away from (not to) the sin or offense that we committed. Merriam Webster defines repentance as a turning from sin and a resolve to reforms one's life. I believe that the way we accomplish this turning away is a combination of renewing our minds as well as crucifying our flesh. That's why The Apostle Paul spoke so much about the process in Romans chapter eight. When you repent for real, you can "walk in the spirit and not fulfill the lust of the flesh." John the Baptist's whole ministry was centered around repentance. It has become such a ministry in the Christian culture that even our penal system adopted its principles. As a matter of fact, we get the word penitentiary from the philosophy of repentance. The most important fact is that we "repent for real" from the heart. It's not an easy task but with the help of the Holy Spirit we can do it. What warms my heart is to know that not only do we have immediate benefits when we repent for real, but God is truly glorified as all the angels in heaven rejoice! Praise God!

Additional Reading: Matthew 4:17, 3:2; Acts 2:38; Luke 15:7, 10

Soul Check

Did you repent for real?

Prayer

Lord Jesus, I confess my sins and repent of my wicked ways.

Day 88

"Out Back"

Psalm 46:1

God is our refuge and strength, a very present help in trouble.

The title of today's devotion is not taken from the famous "Outback Steakhouse," nor is it making any reference to the land down under. No, the definition for today's' title is somewhat slang for "not having any help at all." To give you an example, one may say "when it comes to my finances, I'm out back." It's a term that is understood by the younger generation, especially those in the jail and prison system. Lately, I've been hearing terms that sound very far fetched but actually have meaning to those who are saying them as well as those who are listening. There are many instances in the natural where someone could definitely be "out back." However, when it comes to the spiritual and the things of God, you can never be out back, for the Word of God always has nothing but positive and encouraging advice for all believers. Even when the circumstances or situations in life dictate the worst possible outcome, God still will never leave you "out back." His help is always available, so please check out the Scripture verses for today and let the Holy Spirit comfort and guide you in your time of meditation. Isn't it wonderful to know that we have such a loving heavenly Father who helps us in our time of need and never leaves us out back. Praise God!

Additional Reading: Psalm 121:1-8; Isaiah 41:10, 14; Hebrew 4:16

Soul Check

Do you feel "out back?"

Prayer

Father, thank you that you will never leave me nor forsake me, that you will help me in my time of need and I won't be left "out back!"

Day 89

"But At Midnight"

Acts 16:25

And at midnight, Paul and Silas prayed, and sang praises unto God: and the prisoners heard them.

Back in the early Sixties a contemporary singer name Wilson Pickett had a number one hit called "Midnight Hour." One of the main verses was; "I'm gonna wait until the "midnight hour;" that's when my love comes tumbling down." Usually anything associated with "midnight" has to do with negative occurrences. Party people tend to wait until close to midnight before they go out to have fun. Midnight also refers to the darkest hour of the day. In the natural, it's always equated with the gloomiest time. However, in the spiritual, midnight takes on positive connotations as well. Just think of how the Lord will sometimes wait till the "midnight" hour before He instructs you to do something. So when His hand is in it, it has to have a positive and glorious outcome. Look how Samson performed a miracle at "midnight" (Judges 16:3); and how David rose to praise Him at that time (Psalm 119:62). Other instances are when Boaz discovered Ruth at "midnight" and the Apostle Paul and Silas praying and praising God while in jail. (Ruth 3:8 and Acts 16:25) So you see great things happen for the men and women of God, even at midnight. If you are going through something right now and sense that this is definitely a midnight experience, know that the Lord is there with you.

Additional Reading: Matthew 25:6; Acts 20:7; Luke 11:5

Soul Check

Are you experiencing a "midnight?"

Prayer

Lord, just as you allowed great things to happen through Sampson, David, Boaz, Paul and Silas at "midnight," I believe that you will do the same for me.

Day 90

"Prayer #1"

1 Thessalonians 5:17

Pray without ceasing.

In discussing issues in our 120 days of devotions, I don't want to neglect the topic of prayer. I believe that prayer must be the focal point of our relationship with Christ, for it is our means of communication with our heavenly Father. Since communication is the basis of life, then communicating with God must be at the center of our worship to Him. Dr. Edwin Louis Cole taught us that prayer produces intimacy with the One to whom you are praying, the one that you are praying for and the one you are praying with. Most incarcerated individuals have difficulty praying due to the fact that they are praying to an unseen Person. Some claim that they don't know how to pray or what to pray, yet they have a desire to pray. Well, my advice is similar to that of Pastor Jackie McCullough who says, "When we pray, we need to give ourselves completely, yielding to God physically, intellectually, emotionally and spiritually." My paraphrase is to talk to God just the way you talk and with your whole heart, soul, and body. God understands how we talk so as long as it's from the heart, He will accept and answer our prayers. David gives us a good example of how to pray, what to pray and even when to pray in the Psalms.

Additional Reading: Ephesians 6:18; Luke 18:1; Philippians 4:6

Soul Check

Are you praying without ceasing?

Prayer

Lord, teach me how to pray and what to pray for.

Day 91

"Stop Buckin"

1 Samuel 15:23

For rebellion is as the sin of witchcraft, and stubbornness is as iniquity and idolatry. Because thou has rejected the word of the Lord, he hath also rejected thee from being king.

If you have ever witnessed wild stallions in their natural habitat, you probably have seen them bucking like crazy, especially when they are being broken.. I don't envy the person that has the job of breaking those wild stallions in. The buckin', or breaking in, just seems to be sort of painful. However, the "buckin'" we are talking about today has nothing to do with horses. When you hear someone tell someone else to "stop buckin," what that person is saying is "stop being rebellious and get with the program." Usually it takes on a negative vibe. We could say that "stop buckin" is the exact opposite of obeying or conforming to the said program. Well, when it comes to fulfilling and applying Romans 12:1, 2 to our lives, many of us rebel and continue to live like the world lives. So it's no surprise that the Lord is moving on our hearts to stop buckin and get on with His program (plan) and purpose for our lives. We buck when we don't do what His Word encourages us to do, walk in love and obey the leading of the Holy Spirit. We buck when we treat the Word of God merely as a novel instead of a divinely inspired Word of God! We also buck when we don't have love for one another. Well, I believe that you get the point and realize that its time to stop buckin. We have too much at stake to continue in any rebellious behavior. The Apostle Paul bucked when he kicked against the goads (Acts 9:5), but as soon as he met Jesus, he stopped buckin, and so should we. Praise God!

Additional Reading: Acts 9:3-6; Psalm 78:8; Ezekiel 3:9

Soul Check

Are you "buckin?"

Prayer

Lord, help me to "stop buckin," and let my behavior line up with your Word.

Day 92

"Put Away Childishness"

Ephesians 4:14

That we henceforth be no more children, tossed to and fro, and carried about with every wind of doctrine by the sleight of men, and cunning craftiness, whereby they lie in wait to deceive.

One of the greatest truths I've learned from God's Word is that "He gives us the power to become children of God." What that denotes to me is that this Christian walk is a powerful one (John 1:12), not weak or inferior like the world thinks. And though we are children and will always be children in our relationships with Him, He doesn't want us to remain children. He wants us to grow up and "put away childishness." (See 1 Corinthians 13:11) Many men in our jails and prisons haven't put away childishness and subsequently have become adult adolescents. When you look at some of the characteristics of childish behavior you can see why I write the way I do. Some of them are: 1) A child is the center of their own universe; 2) A child is insensitive to the needs of others; 3) A child demands its own way; 4) A child has a temper tantrum when not catered to; 5) A child is unable to reason; 6) A child is irresponsible in its behavior; 7) A child only responds to concrete authority. So when you look at these characteristics of a child, it should provoke you to put away childishness. God wants us to be childlike, not childish. That's what He means when He says, "Unless you become like a child, you can not enter the Kingdom of God." (Matthew 18:3) Remember as you strive to put away childishness that a child is humble, teachable and dependent. That's the way the Lord wants us to be. Praise God!

Additional Reading: Ephesians 4:11-14; Hebrew 5:12 – 6:2; 1 Corinthians 13:11

Soul Check

Am I childish or childlike?

Prayer

Holy Spirit, teach me to be childlike.

Day 93

"Godly Misfits"

1 Samuel 16:7

But the Lord said unto Samuel, Look not on his countenance, or on the height of his stature; because I have refused him: for the Lord seeth not as man seeth; for man looketh on the outward appearance, but the Lord looketh on the heart.

Have you ever wondered whether God can really use you for His Kingdom purposes or not? I mean that considering His awesomeness and His majesty and then comparing it with our fallibility and human faculties, one might just question such a possibility. However, when it comes to the assignments that the Lord has for His servants, the application, as well as the qualifications He uses differs from what we would use. We tend to look at the outer man (skills, talents, degrees and gifts) while God looks at the heart of a man, so many of us think we don't qualify for service in His Kingdom. But let's take a look at some of the servants He did use. Abraham was old; Jacob was insecure; Joseph was abused; Moses stuttered; Leah was unattractive; Gideon was poor; Samson was codependent; Rahab was immoral; David had an affair and all kinds of family problems; Elijah was suicidal; Jeremiah was depressed; Jonah was reluctant; Naomi was a widow; John the Baptist was eccentric (to say the least); Peter was impulsive and hot-tempered; Martha worried a lot; the Samaritan woman had several failed marriages; Zacchaeus was unpopular; Thomas had doubt; Paul had poor health and Timothy was timid. That is quite a variety of misfits, but God used each of them in His service. I call them "Godly misfits." Now you can stop wondering if you qualify and join Him in the service He has assigned you. Once you do then you can join this Hall of Fame of "Godly misfits." Hallelujah!

Additional Reading: Hebrews 11; 1 Corinthians 1:26-29; John 15:16

Soul Check

Are you a Godly misfit?

Prayer

Lord, thank you that you look at my heart and not my outward appearance.

Day 94

"Radical Praise Team"

2 Chronicles 20:21

And when he had consulted with the people, he appointed singers unto the Lord, and that should praise the beauty of holiness, as they went out before the army, and to say, Praise the Lord; for his mercy endureth for ever.

Most of the choirs and the praise teams we see in the body of Christ are usually made up of 80 to 90 percent women. Men for some reason just don't gravitate to the music department, no matter how musically inclined they are, and sometimes the ones who really want to just are not as musically gifted. In the Old Testament most of the worship responsibilities were filled by men (priests) so it never seemed unusual for a praise team to be all men. Yet, the praise team I'm encouraging you to join is a "radical praise team." This praise team isn't one that entertains you or spends a lot of time trying to pump you up so that you can join them in praising the Lord. No, this type of praise team is truly a radical praise team that is equipped for spiritual warfare. When the Lord sent His servant Jehoshaphat to battle the Ammorites and the Moabites as well as the inhabitants of Seir, He gave him some radical instructions. He told him that he should put the praise and worship team in front of the warriors. There's just something crazy that goes on in the heavenlies when men worship God, because He always responds in a radical way. When the praise and worship team began to sing on Jehoshaphat's command, God set ambushes against the enemies' camp and caused them to slay one another. Now if that's not a radical praise team, I don't know what is! The Lord is looking for men and women to be a part of His end-time "radical praise team." Won't you join Him? Selah

Additional Reading: 2 Chronicles 20:1-24; Acts 16:25-26; Joshua 6:16

Soul Check

Are you part of the "radical praise team?"

Prayer

Holy Spirit. teach me how to radically praise and worship the Lord, thereby equipping me for spiritual warfare.

Day 95

"Keep Moving Forward"

2 Kings 7:3

And there were four leprous men at the entering in of the gate: and they said one to another, Why sit we here until we die?

Having learned that God does everything according to a pattern based on the principles in the Kingdom of God, I began to look for patterns and principles as I studied the Word of God. For instance, I located a pattern such as the one in 2 Corinthians 5:17-20. It states that once we become a new creation, we then receive a word and ministry of reconciliation. Then finally we become ambassadors for Christ. So when I find a pattern like this, I make a note *pat* for pattern and *prin* for principle next to it. My desire is to study all of the patterns and principles in the Word so that I can keep moving forward in my spiritual growth. To be successful in this walk, we must move forward and not backwards. And standing still is not an option. Look at the four lepers in 2 Kings Chapter 7: They are facing a dilemma and must make a decision soon. They know they can't go back or they die. They can't sit still or they die. Yet, there's a 50/50 chance that they will live if they go forward. Once they do decide to keep moving forward, God goes ahead of them and causes confusion in the enemy's camp. So not only do they live, but the enemy's camp is deserted and all of the wealth of the enemy is left intact. You may be facing a dilemma in your spiritual journey right now. You know that you must do something, but until now you didn't know what. Well, if you're like most of us, you can't go backwards, and neither can you stay stagnated, so my suggestion is that you keep moving forward. Thank you, Jesus!

Additional Reading: 2 Kings 7:3-8; Jeremiah 7:24; Exodus 14:14

Soul Check

Are you moving forward?

Prayer

Lord, give me the courage to move forward and to trust that you have gone ahead of me.

Day 96

"Get Your House In Order"

2 Kings 20:1

In those days was Hezekiah sick unto death. And the prophet Isaiah the son of Amoz came to him, and said unto him, Thus saith the Lord, Set thine house in order; for thou shalt die, and not live.

One of the most important assignments we men have as Christians is to "get your house in order." Nothing is even remotely as important (with the exception of not being saved) as this assignment, because when your house isn't in order, then everyone in the household is out of order. The reason I'm focusing on the men in today's devotion is because God has placed man at the head of the household since the beginning of time. He issued His command to Adam first, not Eve, and consequently will hold the man responsible. It's his job to maintain order in the home and to fail to do so puts everything concerning the household in jeopardy. I'm reminded of the story of King Hezekiah who was about to die, and the Lord told him to "get your house in order." Immediately King Hezekiah began to pray and reminded the Lord how he walked with him, so the Lord extended his life for 15 more years. Now, I don't know where you are at in regards to this present life, and I hope that no one is near death as you read this devotion. But whether you are or not, I still encourage you to get your house in order. Pray and ask the Lord for wisdom to help you accomplish this task. Cover your family in the blood of Jesus, and above all things, trust God to help you get your house in order. Praise God!

Additional Reading: 2 Kings 20:1-6; 2 Samuel 17:23; 1 Corinthians 11:3, 8-12; 1 Corinthians 14:40

Soul Check

Is your house in order?

Prayer

Lord, help me to set my house in order.

Day 97

"Ordinary People"

Acts 4:13

Now when they saw the boldness of Peter and John, and perceived that they were unlearned and ignorant men, they marveled; and they took knowledge of them, that they had been with Jesus.

Before I got saved at the age of 37, I thought that all Christians as well as other religious people were super human. Because I hadn't grown up in the church and didn't know anything about God and religion, I assumed that they never get into trouble and always appeared to do right. So when the ideal met the real, I learned that they were just like everyone else, "ordinary people." No matter how the Lord used them to do great exploits, they were still just ordinary people doing extraordinary things. Sometimes our egos get the best of us and cause us to become prideful. We tend to think that we are better than everyone else. Even in the church, we may think we are better than others because we are extremely gifted or do great things in ministry. Well, the Apostle Paul admonishes us "not to think more highly of ourselves then we should." No matter how God chooses to use us, we are still just ordinary people. I like the way Jesus referred to us as "... unprofitable servants, just doing our duty." So don't let the giftings, the offices you desire or the miracles that God has performed in and through you cause you to get a big head. Remember, stay humble, for you are just one of millions of ordinary people that the Lord is using in these end times. Praise Him, for He is worthy!

Additional Reading: Romans 12:3; Luke 17:10; Proverbs 27:2

Soul Check

Are you thinking more highly of yourself because you are saved?

Prayer

Holy Spirit, remind me that I am an ordinary person who can do extraordinary things because of the God I serve.

Day 98

"Forgiveness"

Matthew 6:12

And forgive us our debts, as we forgive our debtors.

One of the most important tenets of our Christian faith next to the love of God and our neighbor is that of forgiveness. I also believe that it is one principle that is highly under- utilized in the body of Christ. Many don't understand the importance of exercising this principle at all costs. There really are no options, reasons or excuses for not obeying this command. Many scriptures highlight having a forgiving spirit just like our Lord and Savior Jesus Christ. I believe that the best example of forgiveness is when Jesus said "Father, forgive them, for they do not know what they do." Stephen echoed this same sentiment when he was about to be stoned to death. How many of us would be willing to forgive the very person or people who are about to bring on our demise? Stephen's act of forgiveness when he said "Lord, do not charge them with this sin," shows us all that we can experience the same level of forgiveness. We can both receive it as well as give it. We are commanded to forgive others just like we want others to forgive us. Remember also that whether those who offended us seek our forgiveness or not, it's still up to us to forgive them so we won't retain their sins. Because today's topic is such a critical ministry of our belief, we will visit it again. So for now make sure you always seek the Lord's forgiveness and always extend the same to others. Thank you, Jesus!

Additional Reading: 1 John 1:9; Colossians 3:13; Psalm 32:1; Luke 23:34; John 20:23

Soul Check

Am I holding any unforgiveness?

Prayer

Father, please forgive me as I forgive those who have sinned against me.

Day 99

"No More Drama"

Romans 12:18

If it be possible, as much as lieth in you, live peaceably with all men.

When someone mentions the word "drama," several things can come to mind based on the context in which it was said. For according to Merriam-Webster Dictionary, drama has several meanings: 1) as literary compositions designed for theatrical presentation; 2) dramatic art, literature or affairs; 3) a series of events involving conflicting forces. The third definition will be the focus of our devotion today. Usually it's the women who create, indulge in and precipitate most of the drama in any given relationship or situation. However, since the correctional system is 87 percent males, it stands to reason that the majority of the drama is done by males. That's why my word of encouragement to those affected by it is, "No more drama." Much of the trouble and stress that is being experienced in this system could be avoided. One would think that in such a controlled environment there would be less drama, but the truth of the matter is that there tends to be more. Most of it is developed based on the attitudes that are displayed. The conflicting forces often fail to consider the consequences of all the drama they are causing, physically, emotionally, mentally and spiritually. Too much drama destroys relationships all around. The key to success is to follow the Word's advice and consider others as better than ourselves. Then you can have an environment with no more drama. Selah

Additional Reading: Romans 12:16-21; 1 Peter 3:8-13; Ephesians 5:1-3; Philippians 2:3

Soul Check

Is there "drama" in your life?

Prayer

Lord, help me to consider others as better than myself.

Day 100

"Wait on Him"

Psalm 37:7, 34

Rest in the Lord and wait patiently for him: fret not thyself because of him who prospereth in his way, because of the man who bringeth wicked devices to pass.

Wait on the Lord, and keep his way, and he shall exalt thee to inherit the Land: when the wicked are cut off, thou shalt see it.

When it comes to our worship, I believe that one aspect that we tend to overlook is that of "waiting on Him." Sometimes I don't think we actually realize just what that entails; plus, most of us think that waiting is passive requiring nothing to be done on our part. However, that's not the case when it comes to waiting on Him. When the Lord instructs us to wait on Him, He isn't implying that we just sit back, relax and kick up our heels. No, He wants us to continue to do what we know to do while we wait on His proceeding Word. I know that this is a lot for brothers and sisters who are incarcerated to swallow, since waiting can be very frustrating, especially when you are waiting to get bailed out, go to court or finish your sentence. I guess the best example of waiting on Him is the job of a waiter. When a waiter or waitress waits on you, they aren't passive or inactive. No, they are constantly checking on you, wanting to know how they can best serve you. And when you don't have any further instructions for them, they just keep checking your table waiting for the next opportunity to serve you. When the Lord tells us to wait on Him, He wants us to continue serving Him until we get more instructions from Him. Many saints do realize that we are waiting on Him when we are waiting on and serving others. Let's not neglect this aspect of our worship and wait on Him with gladness. Hallelujah!

Additional Reading: Psalm 27:14; Isaiah 25:9; Romans 12:7

Soul Check

Am I waiting on the Lord?

Prayer

Holy Spirit, teach me how to wait upon the Lord, and show me the opportunities where I can wait on and serve others.

Day 101

"Unusual Instructions"

Genesis 17:17

Then Abraham fell upon his face, and laughed, and said in his heart, Shall a child be born unto him that is an hundred years old? and shall Sarah, that is ninety years old, bear?

You know, sometimes I really believe that the Lord has the greatest sense of humor and wants us to have one also. Some may think that it goes beyond humor, especially when it comes to the "unusual instructions" that He gives us. Some of the things He asks us to do are truly out of this world, literally. No wonder Sarah laughed when He told Abraham that "by this time next year you will have a son." Being old, barren and somewhat sexually inactive, I'm sure it sounded rather comical to her. And what about the "unusual instructions" He gave Ezekiel when He told him to lie on his left side for 390 days and then on his right side for another 40 days. Also He said that He was going to tie (restrain him) so that he couldn't move during this time. As though that wasn't enough, He then tells him to "cook his food with human dung." Ezekiel must have thought the Lord was definitely joking. What about His "unusual instructions" to Jehoshaphat? Go out to battle with the Assyrians, but don't put the warriors up front; put the praise & worship team there. Surely the things He had Jesus do must qualify for the category of unusual instructions. My point is that no matter how strange or inconceivable the instructions that the Lord gives you might be, just obey them. As a matter of fact, I would personally question some of them if they weren't indeed "unusual instructions." Glory to God!

Additional Reading: Genesis 18:12, 14; Ezekiel 4:1-17; 2 Chronicles 20:17-20; John 21:25

Soul Check

Has the Lord given you "unusual instructions?"

Prayer

Lord, help me to obey when You give "unusual instructions!"

Day 102

"Expectations"

Acts 16:25-26

And at midnight Paul and Silas prayed, and sang praises unto God: and the prisoners heard them. And suddenly there was a great earthquake so that the foundations of the prison were shaken: and immediately all the doors were opened, and every one's bands were loosed.

I can remember when my daughters, Timika and Jorgina, and daughter-in-law Erika were each expecting the birth of their first child. Our families were extremely excited about the births, and their "expectations" were real high. First, they were expecting a smooth delivery with no complications. Secondly, they were expecting a healthy child. Thirdly, they were expecting to create a warm loving home environment for the children. Finally, their expectations for the mom and dad as responsible parents would come into play at the birth of this child. Our families' "expectations" were creating an atmosphere for miracles to occur. Expectations are doing so in the natural based on the obvious, while some of their "expectations" have spiritual significance. When we expect God to fulfill His Word and His promises to us, our faith creates the atmosphere for miracles. Just look at the woman with an issue of blood; she created an atmosphere for a miracle when her faith cause her to confess, "If I can just touch the hem of His garment..". We too can create the atmosphere for miracles through our expectations. Meditate on where you could use a miracle; then unleash your faith, which consists of your expectations. and let the Lord work wonders on your behalf. Hallelujah!

Additional Reading: Acts 2:1-7; Acts 12:11, Luke 8:5-8; Luke 8:43-44

Soul Check

What are your "expectations?"

Prayer

Lord, I expect for You to move on my behalf as I delight myself in Your Word.

Day 103

"Watch Your Mouth"

James 3:6

And the tongue is a fire, a world of iniquity: so is the tongue among our members that it defileth the whole body, and setteth on the fire the course of nature: and it is set on fire of hell.

Though I'm no expert, nor have I (or anyone I know) done a survey on the arguments and fights that go on in the prison system, yet I feel very confident in the claim I'm about to share. For I believe that well over 80 percent of conflicts have erupted based on what someone said. Most of the time, the "someone" is our own selves. James wrote all about this in the fourth chapter of the letter to the 12 tribes that were scattered abroad. Not only does he tell them the source of all conflicts but also warns them to "watch your mouth," because this is the instrument used to ignite those fiery conflicts. That's why Jesus explained to us that it's not what goes in the mouth that defiles a man, but things such as evil thoughts, murders, adulteries, fornications, thefts, false witness and blasphemies. I believe that Jesus was telling them in so many words to "watch your mouth." The Proverbs say that "the power of death and life is in the tongue." James cautions us about the dangers of the tongue, that it is virtually impossible to tame. He calls it "an ungodly evil," then goes on to say that with it we bless God yet curse man who was created in God's image. So I encourage all of us to please watch your mouth. Think before you speak, for this is a true sign of spiritual maturity. Selah.

Additional Reading: James 3:5-10; James 4:1; Matthew 15:17-20; Psalm 140:3; Matthew 15:11; Proverbs 18:21

Soul Check

Watch your mouth!

Prayer

Holy Spirit. I pray that I will not allow my tongue to be a tool in the hand of the enemy.

Day 104

"Guard Your Heart"

Proverbs 16:1, 9

The preparations of the heart in man, and the answer of the tongue, is from the Lord. A man's heart deviseth his way: but the Lord directed his steps.

As I was conversing with an inmate recently, he became rather upset when we started talking about the heart. I mentioned to him the importance of "guarding your heart," because the Bible says "as a man thinketh in his heart, so is he." He angrily responded that he doesn't believe that we think with our hearts but only with our minds. Rather than debate or argue with him, I simply shared some Scriptures with him, praying that the Holy Spirit would reveal to him the vital role the heart plays in our lives.

Since the heart is the seat of all motivations and desires, then we need to watch what we feed it. Jesus himself talked about that which proceeds out of the mouth. The flood of Noah's day was just a direct result of the evil thoughts of man's heart. I'm sure that the Lord knows the difference between the heart and the mind and where our thoughts come from. But I also understand that "the heart is deceitful above all things ..." The Proverbs clearly warn us to "guard our heart, for out of it are the issues of life. Based on these few Scriptures, there is no room for questioning whether the heart has the capacity to think or not. Now I see why the Lord wants to give us a "new heart" the moment we are saved. A heart must be able to think if it has to plan his ways. So whatever you do, do all you can to guard your heart. Amen.

Additional Reading: Matthew 12:34; Proverbs 23:7; Genesis 6:5; Matthew 15:19-20; Jeremiah 17:9; Proverbs 4:23; Ezekiel 36:26

Soul Check

Are you guarding your heart?

Prayer

Lord, protect my heart, and help me guard it.

Day 105

"Don't Walk, Stand, or Sit"

Psalm 1:1, 2

Blessed is the man that walketh not in the counsel of the ungodly ,nor standeth in the way of sinners, nor sitteth in the seat of the scornful. But his delight is in the law of the Lord, and in his law doth he meditate day and night.

Have you ever wondered how you got yourself in a certain predicament that caused you to develop a habit? It's like you wake up one day in a severe crisis and you're lost for how or why you are there. Thirty days ago you were doing just fine; then all of a sudden, you're somewhere you don't want to be. Well, it's a subtle ploy of the enemy. The Psalm for today's devotion shows just how this scheme works. It starts when you allow yourself to "take a walk" with the enemy. Then as you are casually walking along, his deception comes in, and you "stand around" listening to his lies, sometimes subconsciously. Then before you know it, you are "sitting down" with the enemy. This is when the habit starts to form and your behavior begins to change. So today's devotion encourages us not to walk, stand or sit with the sinner, ungodly or scornful person. As a matter of fact, this same Psalm says we are blessed when we don't. So it's all about who you fellowship with and what you allow yourself to be subject to. Even the Apostle Paul warned us against being unequally yoked with non-believers. When we follow these Biblical instructions, we can avoid falling into this pattern of ungodly fellowship. Plus, you won't wake up one morning in a predicament you don't want to be in. Yes, saints, don't walk, stand or sit with those who don't know your God! Hallelujah

Additional reading: 2 Corinthians 6:14; Proverbs 4:14; Jeremiah 15:17

Soul Check

Who are you walking, standing or sitting with today?

Prayer

Lord, I purpose in my heart not to walk, stand or sit with the ungodly. Help me recognize the ploy of the enemy.

Day 106

"Take Care of the Children"

Matthew 18:3

And he said, Verily I say unto you, Except ye be converted, and become as little children, ye shall not enter into the kingdom of heaven.

Sometimes I wonder to what degree our selfishness grows when we experience a season of incarceration. I'm constantly encouraging the brothers to stop demanding for their people-- whether it's their wives, girlfriends or their mamas--to do more for them than they are able. Since they aren't cognizant of the amount of pressure that they put on their loved ones, I tell them to at least "take care of the children." Instead of demanding some canteen money or jacking the phone bill up, find a way to take care of the children. Yes, even from the inside there's something you can do to help take care of the children, though maybe not to the degree you would like to or are used to. But rest assured that to most children, anything from Daddy speaks volumes and is more important than that from another source. A homemade card, a dollar, a short note or a printed envelope tells a child that you really care about them. So instead of trying to make your stay more comfortable to the point where you don't mind being incarcerated, take care of the children. Not only is the child (ren) blessed but so are the mothers of those children. And believe it or not, when you take care of the children. you are automatically blessed beyond your wildest dreams. Blessings that are eternal. Selah!

Additional Reading: Psalm 127:3-5; John 1:12; Proverbs 13:22

Soul Check

Fathers, are you taking care of your children?

Prayer

Father, forgive me for neglecting my children. Holy Spirit, teach me to take care of my children.

Day 107

"Wired for Fellowship"

Genesis 2:18

And the Lord God said, It is not good that man should be alone; I will make him a help meet for him.

William loves to be alone and at times becomes very rebellious when forced into the main prison population. Because he is still struggling with his sexuality, he feels more comfortable staying to himself. He desires to change but constantly struggles with the flesh versus the spirit. He has become so self-centered and independent until it's a constant challenge to change. Several times I've tried to encourage him to fellowship with the believers no matter how he feels. I've even shared with him from Scriptures how we all are "wired for fellowship" from the very beginning. As a matter of fact, it was our heavenly Father's desire for fellowship that inspired Him to create us. Take a moment to study the Scripture verses for today, and pray for a fresh revelation on how we are truly "wired for fellowship." Isolation only makes one seek his own interest. Yes, it's good to get alone with God on a regular basis, but not at the expense of fellowship. Personal Bible studies, seasons of prayer and fasting all have their place in our spiritual disciplines, yet we must maintain a proper balance with fellowship. Jesus went by himself to pray to the Father, but He always returned to His disciples. Understand the importance of being "wired for fellowship," and allow it to bless your walk with God. Hallelujah!

Additional Reading: Proverbs 18:1; Hebrews 10:25; Acts 2:42; 1 John 1:3

Soul Check

Are you lacking fellowship?

Prayer

Lord, help me to partake in Godly fellowship and not isolate myself.

Day 108

"Fear and Faith – Same Definition?"

Hebrews 11:1, 6

Now faith is the substance of things hoped for, the evidence of things not seen. But without faith it is impossible to please him: for he that cometh to God must believe that he is, and that he is a rewarder of them that diligently seek him.

According to Merriam-Webster's Dictionary, fear and faith have different definitions, as well as synonyms. For instance, fear is 1) to have a reverent awe of (God); 2) to be afraid of ; 3) to be apprehensive. That's fear the verb, whereas fear the noun is as follows: 1) an unpleasant often strong emotion caused by expectation or awareness of danger; 2) anxious concern; 3) profound reverence especially toward God. Some of the synonyms are dread, fright, alarm, panic, and terror. Faith's definition is 1) allegiance to duty or a person; 2) belief or trust in God; 3) a system of religious beliefs. However, spiritually speaking, fear and faith have the same definition, which is believing that something you cannot see will come to pass. The only difference is, one is negative and one is positive. The spiritual aspect is of utmost importance, due to the fact that both greatly affect our belief system. Because there is such a thin line between "fear and faith," we need to test the spirit behind each to ascertain which one is operating in our lives at any given moment. Fear will create doubts and steal all of your blessings. Faith will cause you to move mountains that will glorify the Lord. So the next time you sense your faith being challenged, check to make sure you're not being fearful. Remember "fear and faith" have the same definition spiritually, so always walk in faith.

Additional Reading: Hebrews 4:2; 2 Corinthians 5:7; Proverbs 29:25; 2 Timothy 1:7

Soul Check

Fear or faith – how are you walking?

Prayer

Holy Spirit, teach how to walk by faith and not by fear.

Day 109

"The Things of Men"

Galatians 5:19-21 Amplified

Now the doings (practices) of the flesh are clear (obvious): they are immorality, impurity, indecency. Idolatry, sorcery, enmity, strife, jealousy, anger (ill temper), selfishness, divisions (dissensions), party spirit (factions, sects with peculiar opinions, heresies). Envy, drunkenness, carousing, and the like, I warn you beforehand, just as I did previously, that those who do such things shall not inherit the kingdom of God..

After reading Pastor Bill Johnson's book, "The Supernatural Power of a Transformed Mind," I began to look at "the things of men" and "the things of God" in a whole new perspective. I will focus on the things of men in today's devotion and the things of God in tomorrow's lesson. Jesus once said to the religious leaders of His day, that … "you have made the commandment of God of no effect by your tradition." (Matthew 15:6) So our traditions fall into the category of the things of men. Our attitudes and behaviors do also. What about the legalistic burdens they place on the backs of men? We know for certain that the "works of the flesh" listed in Galatians, chapter 5, are definitely on the list of the things of men. Some things that aren't included in the Galatians list are lying, pride and gambling, as well as unsound doctrine. There is also a list in 2 Timothy the third chapter that describes some things of men that really deserve our attention, such as men being "lovers of themselves, lovers of money, traitors and having a form of godliness." I guess I could go on and list thousands of things that could be considered the things of men. However, I'll sum up this devotion by saying that any fleshly or carnal, as well as natural thing can be listed, including man's thoughts. Let's just remember that all things that aren't from God have their source in man-- even the ones that are influenced by Satan. That's why Jesus said, "Get behind me, satan … for you are mindful of "the things of men."

Additional Reading: 2 Timothy 3:1-5; Matthew 16:23; 1 Corinthian 6:9-11

Soul Check

Am I being influenced by the "things of men?"

Prayer

Holy Spirit expose areas in my life that are influenced by the "things of men."

Day 110

"The Things of God"

1 Corinthians 2:9-12

But as it is written, Eye hath not seen, nor ear heard, neither have entered into the heart of man, the things which God hath prepared for them that love him. But God hath revealed them unto us by his Spirit: for the Spirit searcheth all thing, yea the deep things of God. For man knoweth the things of a man, save the spirit of man which is in him? Even so the things of God knoweth no man but the Spirit of God.

After reviewing yesterday's devotion, we can safely say that the things of men have a fleshly, earthly or demonic source. So it makes sense that "the things of God" must have a totally different source, which is heaven. When we look to heaven with the mind of Christ, our heavenly Father will show us the pattern of things in heaven. The things of God, having their source completely in the Almighty, are revealed to those who walk in obedience and obey His commands. (See John 14:21) Looking heavenward, we can see the obvious as well as the "deep things of God," as the Spirit reveals them. The obvious includes light, peace, great love and forgiveness. Things of God also include order, mercy, favor from God, healing, deliverance, and abundant life, as well as continual praise and worship for our God. I would be redundant if I tried to list all of the obvious things of God, so I'll simply say that everything that is good and perfect comes from Him, and there's nothing negative with or from Him. As for the deep things of God, they are only revealed by His Spirit (1 Corinthians 2:10) and go way beyond what we could ever ask or imagine. They are things which go contrary to all human intellect, logic or reasoning. They are the things of God which take that which is crooked and make it straight, or that which is unclean and make it clean, as well as that which is invisible and make it visible. Only God can take that which is from the guttermost to the uttermost! Thank God for "the things of God."

Additional Reading: 1 Corinthians 2:9-14; Matthew 16:23; John 3:12; James 1:17

Soul Check

Do I have the revelation of what "the things of God" are?

Prayer

Holy Spirit, reveal to me "the things of God".

Day 111

"Are You in Good Hands?"

Isaiah 49:16

Behold, I have graven thee upon the palms of my hands; thy walls are continually before me.

This slogan very well may be the claim to fame by Allstate, the insurance company. However, I don't think they would mind if I use it to share a Biblical truth, because somewhere along your Christian journey you are going to ask yourself, "Are you in good hands?" It's not that we are questioning our relationship with the Lord, but rather our present position with Him at certain times. Because there are so many challenges and trials facing us constantly, our faith is often challenged too. Sometimes we feel so abandoned that we feel like David when he penned the 22nd Psalm or Jesus when He cried out on the Cross the words, "My God, My God, why have you forsaken me?" ... They both rose above those feelings, and we must do the same, knowing that no matter what we feel or think, He promises to never leave or forsake us. Especially when we are incarcerated, we sometimes through feelings of loneliness wonder, "Am I in good hands?" Well, I want to encourage you to study Isaiah 49:16 so you will know that you are in better hands than Allstate. Take those moments of loneliness as opportunities to be with the One who would never abandon you. Then you'll never again question yourself concerning, "Are you in good hands." Praise God!!!

Additional Reading: Hebrews 13:5; Matthew 28:20; Joshua 1:5, 6, 9

Soul Check

Am I in good hands?

Prayer

Holy Spirit, help me to understand that I am truly engraved upon His hands, and my walls are continually before Him. Therefore, I am in good hands!

Day 112

"Whole Lot of Shakin' Going On"

Hebrews 12:26, 27

Whose voice then shook the earth: but now he hath promised, saying, Yet once more I shake not the earth only, but also heaven. And this word, Yet once more, signifieth the removing of those things that are shaken, as of things that are made, that those things which cannot be shaken may remain.

If you grew up in the late Fifties and early Sixties like I did, your entire life was pretty much under the influence of Rock and Roll. As far as I can recall, there weren't a whole lot of different music categories. Rock and Roll was it. One of the great movers and shakers in the industry was Jerry Lee Lewis, who was known for his outrageous antics and his piano playing style. One of his most notable hits was, "Whole Lot of Shakin' Going On." His reference was to dancing and partying all the time. I must admit that I didn't really pay much attention to the lyrics of most songs, including this one. However, when it comes to the Word of God, I try to pay as much attention as possible to what the Lord is saying to the church and to me in particular. What brought this particular song to mind is that we are presently in a season of shaking. Yes, the church is experiencing a "Whole Lot of Shakin' Going On." Both individuals and families, as well as whole ministries, are confronted with this spiritual shaking, so it's of utmost importance that we check out where we are at spiritually and let go of everything that is not of God and can be shaken. I, for one, would rather let it go than to have it shaken out of me. Do you sense lately a "Whole Lot of Shakin' Going On?" If so, then do what the Holy Spirit is leading you to do, and trust the Lord to keep you safe. Thank you, Jesus!!!

Additional Reading: Haggai 2:6, 7; Joel 3:16; Acts 4:32

Soul Check

Do I have anything that I need to let go of before the shaking of the Lord comes?

Prayer

Lord, I purpose in my heart to heed the leading of the Holy Spirit to remove those things that are displeasing to the Father.

Day 113

"Hidden Treasures"

Exodus 19:5

Now therefore, if ye will obey my voice indeed, and keep my covenant, then ye shall be a peculiar treasure unto me above all people: for all the earth is mine.

When the Lord allows some of His children to go through periods of incarceration, it's usually to get them back on the right track--the track that they had detoured from because of some bad choices they made. He wants us to refocus on Him and the plans He has for our lives. But we sometimes continually focus on our problems, mistakes, and failures of the past. One of our top priorities is to find a way out anyway we can. Yet, the Lord is saying, "Sit still and trust me. I want to bring out those "hidden treasures" that I have deposited in you from the foundation of the world. If I could just get you to focus on Me instead of yourself, I will bring out the greatness that is in you." So many of you men and women have listened to the lie of the enemy, and now it's time to rise up, believe the truth about who you really are. Don't let the past dictate your future, or else the hidden treasures will remain hidden. The enemy knows that correctional facilities are full of hidden treasures. That's why he doesn't want you to discover that you are one of God's treasures and keeps you focusing on the prison culture. When those hidden treasures are uncovered then many pastors, prophets, teachers, lawyers, doctors, artists, evangelists, businessmen, lecturers and many other professionals will come forth to the glory of God! It's time for the release of those hidden treasures. Selah

Additional Reading: Jeremiah 29:11; 2 Corinthians 4:7; Matthew 12:35

Soul Check

What hidden treasure do I have in my earthen vessel?

Prayer

Lord, help me to focus on what you have planned for my life and to discover the hidden treasure within me.

Day 114

"Friendship with the World"

James 4:4

Ye adulterers and adulteresses, know ye not that the friendship of the world is enmity with God? Whosoever therefore will be a friend of the world is the enemy of God.

When we think of friendship, it usually will involve another person or persons. Many of us never even considered a system or institution as being the object of our friendship, yet, James 4:4 says exactly that. The world system as we know it today is so diametrically opposed to the things of God, until we become an enemy of His when we align ourselves with it. The Bible also says that "the world is passing away and its desires with it," so why would we want to become friends with it? The few verses before it tell us that "if we love the world, the love of the Father is not in us." As I write this devotion, I'm mindful of the large percentage of inmates that have developed such a strong "friendship with the world," and I'm praying for a major revival in the prisons and jails. If we would only take a moment to seriously look at all of the negativity and demonic influence in the world, I think we would think twice before going back to this friendship with the world. Even satan knew the consequences of this; that's why he offered Jesus all of kingdoms of the world. The world's system, though it may look good at times, only leads to death. Even though there appears to be opportunities to do good, from a worldly perspective, it always turns out to be a structural evil. So I encourage you to do all you can to maintain your relationship with the Lord and never, never, ever, allow the enemy to entice you to have friendship with the world. Selah

Additional Reading: 1 John 2:15-17; Matthew 4:8; Romans 12:2

Soul Check

Do I have friendship with the world?

Prayer

Lord, help me to let go any alliances that I may have with the world.

Day 115

"Will You Mock God?"

Galatians 6:7

Be not deceived; God is not mocked: for whatsoever a man soweth, that shall he also reap.

Many of us don't use the term "mock" in our everyday vocabulary and conversations. As a matter of fact, most people don't have a clue as to what it means. So let's start off today's devotion with the definition according to Merriam-Webster's Collegiate Dictionary. Mock means 1) to treat with contempt or ridicule; 2) delude; 3) defy; 4) to mimic in sport or derision. According to these definitions, most might say they are innocent of mocking God. Well, I for one, wouldn't dare pass judgment on anyone. However, I would suggest that each and every one of us take a good inventory of our thoughts, behavior and actions before we so quickly acquit ourselves. I'm convinced that many of us don't intentionally mock God, but that doesn't mean we don't do it. If someone asked me, will you mock God, I would answer no, based on the definition and my intentions. Yet I would have to examine myself thoroughly to see if I defied, ridiculed, mimicked or treated spiritual things with contempt. It's not my intention to point any fingers or even get specific in areas where we may have mocked God. I'm sure that there are enough Biblical examples by unbelievers, false prophets, ungodly Shepherds, self-righteous rulers, and others who mock God on a regular basis. You probably even know of some of your contemporaries who do the same. However, the question is not who mocks God, but "Will you mock God?" Pray that the Holy Spirit will guide you and keep you. Hallelujah

Additional Reading: 1 Samuel 17:36; 2 Chronicles 36:16; Matthew 27:29-31

Soul Check

Do I mock God?

Prayer

Holy Spirit, reveal to me areas where I have mocked God.

Day 116

"Just Do It"

James 1:22-25

But be ye doers of the word, and not hearers only, deceiving your own selves. For if any be a hearer of the word, and not a doer, he is like unto a man beholding his natural face in a glass; For he beholdeth himself, and goeth his way, and straightway forgetted what manner of man he was. But whoso looketh into the perfect law of liberty, and continueth therein, he being not a forgetful hearer, but a doer of the work, this man shall be blessed in his deed.

Nike may have coined the phrase, "Just do it" for it's athletic footwear, but I believe that the term actually has it's origin in God. From the very beginning of creation, God has issued commandments, not requests, to man. Those commandments could easily be interpreted as, "Just do it." All throughout the history of mankind, God lets His servants know what He wants and has called them to do; then He basically tells them to "just do it." He never once asks them if they want to do it. Whether it was Noah and the building of the Ark or Abraham leaving his hometown or Moses delivering the Israelites, God never gave them an option. When Jesus was at the wedding in Cana and his mother requested His services, He said "Woman what have I to do with thee, my hour is not yet come." Yet, His mother interpreted that to mean "... just do it." (John 2:4-5) So the point for today's devotion is that whenever we get a command from the Lord to do something, don't question it, but just do it. James tells us to become a doer of the Word and not just a hearer. So no matter what medium the Lord uses to speak to you, don't resist Him, but obey Him. It may be a prompting of the Holy Spirit or an impression upon your heart; it could even be from a dream and definitely from His Word. Whatever the source, when you recognize that it's God, just do it! Glory to God!!!

Additional Reading: Matthew 7:21; Romans 2:13; Genesis 1:28; Matthew 12:47-50

Soul Check

Are you a doer of the Word?

Prayer

Lord, I purpose to be a doer and not just a hearer of your Word.

Day 117

"Cast Your Burdens"

Psalm 55:22

Cast thy burdens upon the Lord, and he shall sustain thee: he shall never suffer the righteous to be moved.

Cast is one of those words in our English language that has several different meanings. So whenever you see this word being used, read it in context so that you get the correct understanding. Cast in the text today means to "throw, fling, to discard or shed." So when the Biblical verse says to "cast your burdens ..." what we are actually being encouraged to do is to throw, fling or discard all of our burdens upon the Lord. It doesn't matter whether they are major or minor burdens. He doesn't discriminate; a burden is a burden. So why is it so difficult for us to obey this command, especially when we are so heavy-laden with burdens while we are incarcerated? Could it be that we think God's arms are too short to reach down and help us? Or maybe we are deceived into thinking that we can handle them better than He? I like to believe that we want to obey the command to "cast your burdens" but we just don't know how. That's when it is critical that we study the Word and trust the Holy Spirit to lead us and teach us. The Lord wants so badly to have us "cast your burdens" so that we don't get so heavy-laden. Let's follow Jesus' invitation to come to Him so that He will give us rest. The Lord doesn't want us to be burdened down with cares of this world that we are powerless to do anything about, unless we do it through Jesus. However, once you do cast your burdens, you will feel one hundred percent better. Thank you, Jesus!!!

Additional Reading: 1 Peter 5:7; Matthew 11:28

Soul Check

Are you casting your burdens upon the Lord?

Prayer

Lord, I cast my burdens upon you this day, and I receive Your rest for me.

Day 118

"Mind Your Own Business"

John 21:25

Peter seeing him saith to Jesus, Lord, and what shall this man do? Jesus saith unto him, If I will that he tarry till I come, what is that to thee? Follow thou me.

I wrote a devotion on how rampant gossiping is in the correctional system. One element that I didn't think to mention when I discussed the reasons for the rise of gossiping among men, was that most of them fail to "mind their own business." This may sound like a harsh rebuke, but I pray that it will be received in the spirit of which it is written. Every devotion that I have written is inspired by the Holy Spirit and shared with a deep compassion for those who are incarcerated and their families. With all of the tension going on in the jails and prisons, it's imperative that everyone mind their own business. Sticking your nose into someone else's affairs can be harmful, especially since you rarely can determine the mindset of those in your surroundings. And we as Christians should avoid meddling in other people's business. As a matter of fact, the Scriptures are clear on the subject. Even Jesus in so many words cautioned Peter to "mind your own business" when Peter questioned Him about John. So much trouble both inside and outside the correctional system can be avoided if we would daily make a conscious effort to mind our own business." As a matter of fact, one of the best ways to avoid this is to concentrate on paying attention to the Father's business. Jesus did that, even at the early age of 12, and so can we. Selah!

Additional Reading: Luke 2:49; Luke 19:13; 1 Timothy 5:13

Soul Check

Are you minding your own business?

Prayer

Holy Spirit, please convict me when I am not minding my own business, and help me attend to the Father's business.

Day 119

"S.A.D.D."

Nehemiah 9:16 & 17

But they and our fathers dealt proudly, and hardened their necks, and hearkened not to they commandments. And refused to obey, neither were mindful of they wonders that thou didst among them; but hardened their necks, and in their rebellion appointed a captain to return to their bondage: but thou art a God ready to pardon, gracious and merciful, slow to anger, and of great kindness, and forsookest them not.

I love to use or make up acronyms whenever I'm teaching, preaching or just writing. Sometimes I use those in existence by adding a letter or two or changing the meaning or simply make up my own. Today's titled devotion doesn't stand for "Students Against Drunk Drivers," but what I call "Spiritual Attention Deficit Disorder." Everyone knows that "A.D.D." is a disorder that keeps one from paying attention or focusing upon someone or something for any length of time. There are numerous reasons why this disorder affects so many people. Yet my focus isn't to discuss the many variables or reasons why so many saints have "Spiritual Attention Deficit Disorder". My purpose for this devotion is mainly to bring attention to the fact that it affects most of us at one time or another. I believe the main reason is that we tend to forget what God has done for us, sometimes immediately after He does some miracle in our lives. The children of Israel were prime examples of forgetting the great things God had done for them. No sooner had they crossed the Red Sea and Moses went up the mountain for further instructions, than they forgot that the Lord had not only parted the Red Sea but also had shown them numerous miracles when He delivered them from Egypt. Now if that's not a classic example of "Spiritual Attention Deficit Disorder," then I don't know what is. Let's pray that the Lord will deliver us from this spiritual disease. Hallelujah!!!

Additional Reading: Nehemiah 9:7-21; Deuteronomy 29:5-9; Psalm 78:7-72

Soul Check

Am I experiencing S.A.D.D.?

Prayer

Holy Spirit, heal me of S.A.D.D., and I will not forget what the Lord delivered me from.

Day 120

"My Mind Stayed (Not Strayed) on Jesus"

Isaiah 26:3

Thou wilt keep him in perfect peace, whose mind is stayed on thee; because he trusteth in thee.

For weeks I have wanted to get to this particular devotion, mainly because it is my heartfelt desire to keep "my mind stayed (not strayed) on Jesus". Over fifteen years ago, I used to attend a Bible study group in Grapevine, Texas called "The Faithful Few." Though everyone attended different congregations, they all had a great love for Jesus as well as for their brothers and sisters in Christ. Every time we would get together, the first song we would sing was, "My Mind Stayed on Jesus." Everyone would take turns singing a verse individually then sing the chorus together. What a fun time we had praising God. Our worship was genuine, and the song became our Bible study's anthem. Little did I know back then that it would be the foundation of my heartfelt desire to worship Him. Even up to this present season in my life, I want to keep my mind stayed (not strayed) on Jesus. Whether I'm working, ministering, relaxing, spending time with my wife and/or children or just fellowshipping with the saints, I always want to keep my mind stayed on Jesus. Especially during my quiet time and prayer time, I seek and desire an intimacy like I have never had before. And because I do, I have experienced fresh revelation and closeness to Him more and more each time. Keeping "my mind stayed (not strayed) on Jesus" has allowed me to witness many miracles and receive many kingdom blessings. Thank you, Jesus!!!

Additional Reading: Colossians 3:2; Hebrews 12:2; Proverbs 16:7

Soul Check

Is my mind stayed or strayed on Jesus?

Prayer

Lord, I purpose in my heart to keep my mind stayed on Jesus.

PROMISE OF HOPE

FOR I KNOW THE THOUGHTS THAT I THINK TOWARD YOU, SAYS THE LORD, THOUGHTS OF PEACE AND NOT OF EVIL, TO GIVE YOU A FUTURE AND A **HOPE**.

THEN YOU WILL CALL UPON ME AND GO AND PRAY TO ME, AND I WILL LISTEN TO YOU.

AND YOU WILL SEEK ME AND FIND ME, WHEN YOU SEARCH FOR ME WITH ALL YOUR HEART.

I WILL BE FOUND BY YOU, SAYS THE LORD, AND I WILL BRING YOU BACK FROM YOUR CAPTIVITY; I WILL GATHER YOU FROM ALL THE NATIONS AND FROM ALL THE PLACES WHERE I HAVE DRIVEN YOU, SAYS THE LORD, AND I WILL BRING YOU TO THE PLACE FROM WHICH I CAUSED YOU TO BE CARRIED AWAY CAPTIVE.

JEREMIAH 29:11-14 NKJV

Scriptures on Hope

You are my hiding place and my shield; I hope in Your word. Psalm 119: 114

Be strong and let your heart take courage, all you who wait for and hope for and expect the Lord! Psalm 31: 24

And now, Lord, what do I wait for and expect? My hope and expectation are in You. Psalm 39: 7

The Lord is my portion or share, says my living being (my inner self); therefore will I hope in Him and wait expectantly for Him. Lamentations 3: 24

But if we hope for what is still unseen by us, we wait for it with patience and composure. Romans 8: 25

For whatever was thus written in former days was written for our instruction, that by [our steadfast and patient] endurance and the encouragement [drawn] from the Scriptures we might hold fast to and cherish hope. Romans 15: 4

Hope deferred makes the heart sick, but when the desire is fulfilled, it is a tree of life. Proverbs 13: 12

Why are you cast down, O my inner self? And why should you moan over me and be disquieted within me? Hope in God and wait expectantly for Him, for I shall yet praise Him, Who is the help of my [sad] countenance, and my God.
Psalm 43: 5

But I will hope continually, and will praise You yet more and more.
Psalm 71: 14

By having the eyes of your heart flooded with light, so that you can know and understand the hope to which He has called you, and how rich is His glorious inheritance in the saints (His set-apart ones). Ephesians 1: 18

But Christ (the Messiah) was faithful over His [own Father's] house as a Son [and Master of it]. And it is we who are [now members] of this house, if we hold fast and firm to the end our joyful and exultant confidence and sense of triumph in our hope [in Christ]. Hebrews 3: 6

Having [the same] hope in God which these themselves hold and look for, that there is to be a resurrection both of the righteous and the unrighteous (the just and the unjust). Acts 24: 15

To whom God was pleased to make known how great for the Gentiles are the riches of the glory of this mystery, which is Christ within and among you, the Hope of [realizing the] glory. Colossians 1: 27

May the God of your hope so fill you with all joy and peace in believing [through the experience of your faith] that by the power of the Holy Spirit you may abound and be overflowing (bubbling over) with hope. Romans 15: 13

Happy (blessed, fortunate, enviable) is he who has the God of [special revelation to] Jacob for his help, whose hope is in the Lord his God. Psalm 146: 5

So let us seize and hold fast and retain without wavering the hope we cherish and confess and our acknowledgement of it, for He Who promised is reliable (sure) and faithful to His word. Hebrews 10: 23

[Now] we have this [hope] as a sure and steadfast anchor of the soul [it cannot slip and it cannot break down under whoever steps out upon it--a hope] that reaches farther and enters into [the very certainty of the Presence] within the veil. Hebrews 6: 19

I will thank You and confide in You forever, because You have done it [delivered me and kept me safe]. I will wait on, hope in and expect in Your name, for it is good, in the presence of Your saints (Your kind and pious ones). Psalm 52: 9

So that we who first hoped in Christ [who first put our confidence in Him have been destined and appointed to] live for the praise of His glory!
Ephesians 1: 12

[There is] one body and one Spirit--just as there is also one hope [that belongs] to the calling you received Ephesians 4: 4

Yes, let none who trust and wait hopefully and look for You be put to shame or be disappointed; let them be ashamed who forsake the right or deal treacherously without cause. Psalm 25: 3

Wait and hope for and expect the Lord; be brave and of good courage and let your heart be stout and enduring. Yes, wait for and hope for and expect the Lord. Psalm 27: 14

But we belong to the day; therefore, let us be sober and put on the breastplate (corslet) of faith and love and for a helmet the hope of salvation. 1 Thessalonians 5: 8

Awaiting and looking for the [fulfillment, the realization of our] blessed hope, even the glorious appearing of our great God and Savior Christ Jesus (the Messiah, the Anointed One). Titus 2: 13

But we do [strongly and earnestly] desire for each of you to show the same diligence and sincerity [all the way through] in realizing and enjoying the full assurance and development of [your] hope until the end. Hebrews 6: 11

Praised (honored, blessed) be the God and Father of our Lord Jesus Christ (the Messiah)! By His boundless mercy we have been born again to an ever-living hope through the resurrection of Jesus Christ from the dead. 1 Peter 1: 3

So brace up your minds; be sober (circumspect, morally alert); set your hope wholly and unchangeably on the grace (divine favor) that is coming to you when Jesus Christ (the Messiah) is revealed. 1 Peter 1: 13

You will guard him and keep him in perfect and constant peace whose mind [both its inclination and its character] is stayed on You, because he commits himself to You, leans on You, and hopes confidently in You.
Isaiah 26: 3

But as for me, I will look to the Lord and confident in Him I will keep watch; I will wait with hope and expectancy for the God of my salvation; my God will hear me. Micah 7: 7

It is good that one should hope in and wait quietly for the salvation (the safety and ease) of the Lord. Lamentations 3: 26

May the God of your hope so fill you with all joy and peace in believing [through the experience of your faith] that by the power of the Holy Spirit you may abound and be overflowing (bubbling over) with hope. Romans 15: 13

Prayer of Salvation

Dear God,

I know that I have done many sinful deeds. I know that no one can be justified before You by keeping commandments or doing good works because no one can be perfect. I believe that You came to Earth as a man, Jesus Christ. I believe Jesus took upon Himself the sins of the whole world when He was crucified and physically died on a cruel cross at Calvary. I believe Jesus Christ was buried. I believe in my heart that on the third day You, God, physically raised Jesus bodily from the dead. I believe Jesus ascended to Heaven and sat down at Your right hand where He reigns as my Advocate.

I believe that You, God the Father, Jesus Christ the Son and the Holy Spirit are one God. I thank Jesus for taking away my sins forever. I believe Jesus Christ is my Lord and Savior. I believe You will send the Holy Spirit to live within me. I believe I am born again in the Spirit and will now have eternal life with You. Thank You, God, for forgiving me and giving me everlasting life.

In the name of Jesus Christ I pray, Amen.

I want to record the date that I prayed to confess with my mouth the Lord Jesus and believe in my heart that God raised Him from the dead.

"Yes, I just prayed to confess Jesus Christ as my Lord and Savior."

Name: _____ Date: _____

"Heavenly Father, You are the source of all wisdom, You are the source of all Truth".

Open my mind.

Fill me with revelation knowledge.

Fill me with wisdom from above.

Don't challenge me but change me by the renewing of my mind.

Transform my life.

I thank You for it.

I pray for my brethren that they will change while I change; and we will leave this place a new creature, in Jesus' name.

And I will know, what is thy good, acceptable, and perfect will of God for me.

I am ready to change.

I AM ready to change.

I AM READY to change.

I AM READY TO change.

I AM READY TO CHANGE.

I AM READY TO CHANGE.

DECLARATION

THAT THEY MAY BE CALLED OAKS OF RIGHTEOUNESS [**LOFTY, STRONG, AND AMAGNIFICIENT, DISTINGUISED FOR UPRIGHTNESS, JUSTICE, AND RIGHT STANDING WITH GOD**]. THE PLANTING OF THE LORD, THAT HE MAY BE GLORIFIED.

AND THEY SHALL REBUILD THE ANCIENT RUINS, THEY SHALL RISE UP THE FORMER DESOLATIONS AND RENEW THE RUINED CITIES, THE DEVASTATIONS OF MANY GENERATIONS.

BUT YOU SHALL BE CALLED THE PRIESTS OF THE LORD; PEOPLE WILL SPEAK OF YOU AS THE MINISTERS OF GOD, YOU SHALL EAT THE WEALTH OF THE NATIONS, AND THE GLORY [**ONCE THAT OF YOUR CAPTORS**] SHALL BE YOURS.

INSTEAD OF YOUR [**FORMER**] SHAME YOUR SHALL HAVE A TWO FOLD RECOMPENSE; INSTEAD OF DISHONOR AND REPROACH [**YOUR PEOPLE**] SHALL REJOICE IN THEIR PORTION, [**THEREFORE IN THEIR LAND THEY SHALL POSSESS DOULBLE WHAT THEY HAD FOREFIETED**]; EVERLASTING JOY SHALL BE THEIRS.

ISAIAH 61:31 3, 4, 67, 7 AMPLIFIED